WOMEN EMPOWERMENT
Through Panchayati Raj Institutions

About the Author

Dr. Minni Thakur is presently working as a Reader & Head of Department of Political Science in R.N.A.R. College, Samastipur, Bihar. She is also serving as a counsellor in Post Graduate and undergraduate courses in IGNOU. Being a social activist she has keen interest in women problems and she is coordinating Women Development Career Course of U.G.C. in her department. She has attended and presented papers in two dozen national and international seminars and conferences of interdisciplinary subjects and her many works on women empowerment and political science have been published in national and international journals. She has got control over the role of women in PRIs and had organized a national conference on the topic. She is an expert in Panchayati Raj Institution and women studies. She had recently completed minor research project on Political Role of Women and a book has been published by her on 'Social, Political and Economic Ideas of Raja Ram Mohan Roy' also.

Women Empowerment

Through Panchayati Raj Institutions

Minni Thakur

CONCEPT PUBLISHING COMPANY PVT. LTD.,
NEW DELHI-110 059

ISBN-13: 978-81-8069-680-0

First Published 2010

Published and Printed by

Concept
Since 1974

Concept Publishing Company Pvt. Ltd.
Regd. Office:
A/15-16, Commercial Block, Mohan Garden
New Delhi-110059 (India)
Phones : 25351460, 25351794, *Fax* : 091-11-25357109
Email : publishing@conceptpub.com
Website: www.conceptpub.com

Editorial Office:
H-13, Bali Nagar, New Delhi-110 015, India.

Cataloging in Publication Data-- *Courtesy:* D.K. Agencies (P) Ltd. <docinfo@dkagencies.com>

Thakur, Minni.
Women empowerment through panchayati raj institutions / Minni Thakur.
p. cm.
Study conducted in Samastipur District of Bihar, India.
Includes bibliographical references (p.).
Includes index.
ISBN 13: 9788180696800

1. Panchayat--India--Samastipur (District) 2. Rural women--Political activity--India--Samastipur (District) I. Title.

DDC 320.80954123 22

In the loving memory of my beloved mother Late Mrs. Malti Thakur

Dedicated to

Dr. Maheshwara Nand Thakur
(Father)
Forbesganj

Preface and Acknowledgements

Women play a significant and crucial role in all aspects of society, from Village level to National level, but they are not provided their actual share in any process of the society. Especially in political process, lack of decision making is seen everywhere in the state. This is the reason that till 14th parliamentary election in India only 13 per cent women had been given tickets and only 9.6 per cent had won. The Women's Reservation Bill is still pending. It is unfortunate that because of centuries of inertia, ignorance and conservatism the actual and potential role of women in the society has been ignored and preventing them from making their rightful contribution to society and nation.

Many works have been done on women's participation in political process, but there is a lack of original work based on data and emperical study. Most of these works are based on the role of women in the freedom movement and electoral processes. There is a growing consciousness to recognize women's autonomy and their capacity to act as full citizen. Now their role in social, political and economic context has to be understood in the right context.

The study is an attempt to understand the role played by women in the rural environment, especially in Samastipur district of Bihar. The observation had been done on the political awareness and conciousness of rural women of the district before the enactment of the Bihar Panchayati Raj Act, 2006 and after its enactment in which 50 per cent seats have been reserved for women in PRIs. It was observed that before the enforcement of the Act, the women of this district had low consciousness of political activities. They felt politics a dirty game and wanted to be aloof from this game, but after enforcement of this Act 50 per cent posts in all categories were occupied by the women and it opened the all frontal channels for their political awareness and decision making capacities. It is also indicated that caste, class, religion and culture, the existing patriarchic practices etc. play crucial role in determining the position of women in the region. It is also tried for developing strategies for combating the forces operating against participation of women.

The completion of this work is made possible only through the help and inspiration of various people and organizations. I express my heartful gratitude to all well-wishers and helpers for this holy contribution. In this context I am expressing my heartiest gratitude to University Grants Commission, Kolkata for providing financial assistance and guidance for this project work. I am expressing my best gratitude to Dr. M.N. Pandey, Principal of the college, who always made me to believe that I could do better. Without his co-operation, encouragement and supervision, it would have been difficult on my part to complete this work in stipulated period. My father Dr. M. Thakur, Forbesganj has been always with me to promote and increase in the pursuits of learning. My brother Dr. Manau Mahesh, sister Smt. Manju Thakur have also sincerely inspired me for this work.

I take the opportunity to thank Dr. Naresh Kumar Thakur, Dr. Basant Kumar Rai and Sri T.N. Sinha, B.A.S., (Retd.) for their help and co-operation to me. I am also grateful to the members of the National Library, Kolkata, Raja Ram Mohan Roy Library, Sinha Library, Patna, A.N. Sinha Library, Delhi, Central Library, L.N.M.U., Darbhanga. I am also expressing my heartiest gratitude to the staff of Block offices and collectorial staff in the District. The then D.M. Sri Maheshwar Pd. Singh is also in my memory for his kind help in data collection and other official support. I am highly grateful to Dr. R.S. Ojha, (Retd.) Professor of Psychology and Dr. R.B. Mandal, Professor of Geography for their help rendered by them in the planning of the work.

I personally felt that the findings of the study will sensitise and conscientize the policy makers, planners, administrators, teachers and PRIs members for empowering rural women as beneficiaries of this research, training and extension programmes.

Lastly, I also wish to record my gratitude to all those who provided any kind of help during the study period.

Thanks.

Minni Thakur

Contents

1

Introduction

Problem

Our Constitution opens many channels for the development and empowerment of women, economically, socially and politically. The Preamble of the Constitution, the chapters of Fundamental Rights, Directive Principles of State Policies etc., are the specific objectives of this purpose. These constitutional provisions are meant to empower 48.9 per cent women population in India. Many government and non-government agencies are working for the development of women but in practice we find a wide gap between the stated social objectives and achievement, between the legal framework and imperical realities, between the symbolism and actuality. The national and state averages indicated rapid improvement in literacy, education and political participation of women. These trends show the success achieved by a very small group of women. The position of the majority is not satisfactory. There are problems which prevent an average number of women from enjoying their rights and performing their multiple roles in society, especially in politics, women's participation is not satisfactory. Though in freedom movement women played a significant role in the leadership of honourable Mahatma Gandhi. Mahatma Gandhi believed that women had a positive role to play in the reconstruction of society and that the recognition of their equality was an essential step to bring about social justice. But after independence, their participation in different political organizations is not more than ten per cent.

The following Table presents the actual position of women in different general elections.

Table 1.1: Actual Position of Women in Different General Elections

General Election	*No. of Women Elected*	*Percentage*
First	22	4.4
Second	27	5.4
Third	34	6.7
Fourth	31	5.9
Fifth	22	4.2
Sixth	22	3.4
Seventh	19	5.1
Eighth	28	8.1
Ninth	44	5.29
Tenth	28	7.02
Eleventh	34	7.36
Twelfth	40	8.07
Thirteenth	44	9.02
Fourteenth	49	8.25

Soures: Census of India 2001.

The figure in different elections shows a low representation of women in political process. In the sixth general election out of total number of contestants of 2439 only 70 were women and in the fourteenth general election out of total contestants of 59435 only, 355 were women. Though their number is increasing but the growth is very slow and it is also studied that most of the women contestants belong to political or rich families who were of strong background. The political status of women can be judged by the level of their participation, their representation and share in decision making processes. It is very low not only in Samastipur district of Bihar but in whole of India also. There are various reasons for low participation of women in general and in Samastipur district particular, they are:

1. The existence of gender division of labour which limits the role of women to the domestic sphere while extends men's role to the public world.

2. The cultural socialisation which views women as being socialised into feminine and non-competitive roles that do not accord with political activities. It upholds the view that politics is a competitive activity and a dirty game, hence it is meant for men.
3. Women usually lack resources like education, employment, social assistance, political awareness and the male dominated society takes advantages of it.

The credit goes to 73rd and 74th Constitutional Amendment Act in 1992 as Panchayati Raj Act, which not only, provided autonomy to the grassroots but it also provided reservation of one-third of seats for women in every panchayat and municipality, not less than one-third seats shall be reserved for women belonging to scheduled castes and scheduled tribes. This may be allotted by rotation from the constituency to constituency. The present government of Bihar, in 2006 election of Panchayati Raj Institution, had reserved fifty per cent seats for women of all categories. Perhaps, Bihar is the first state to introduce reservation for fifty per cent seats in local bodies' institutions election. Fifty per cent reservation of seats for women in local bodies through acts had opened a channel in the power structure for women from different strata of the society. The new entrants are large in number and they have to play a vital role in the given structure. Till the enactment of the 73rd and 74th Amendments no one was sure about the role to be played by the women in the process of development of the society and women themselves.

In Bihar PRIs election was held in 2001 after a gap of 22 years, in which women from different classes of society won 44815 seats, respectively. It was not possible before the enactment of the Amendments. In Samastipur district alone, 1892 female members won in the three tier structure of PRIs. In the election of 2006, the senario was totally changed, because the present Government of Bihar had reserved fifty per cent seats in PRIs election. Even single post of Mukhia and Sarpanch was also reserved, which was not reserved in 2001 election. The following Table shows the actual number of women in PRIs in Bihar and Samastipur District:

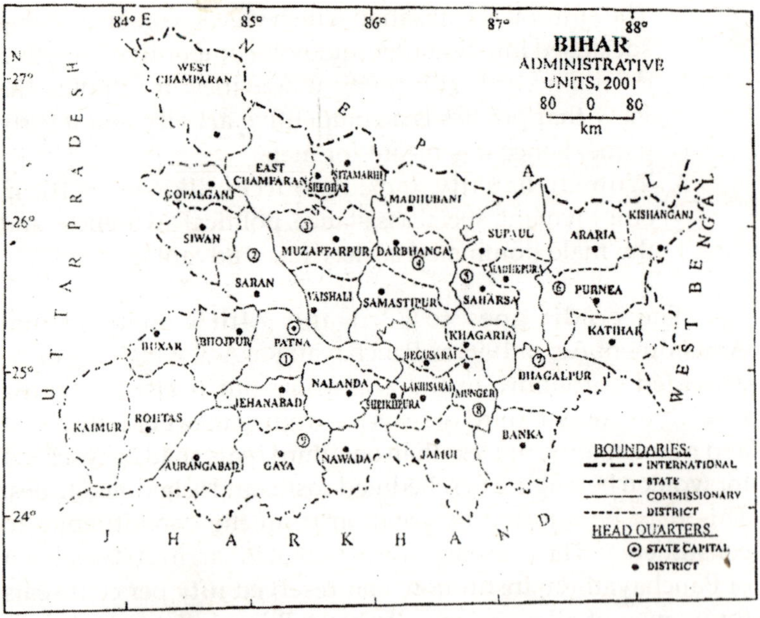

Table 1.2: Recent Status of PRIs in Bihar at Samastipur

Sl. No.	*Name of Post*	*Bihar*	*Samastipur*
1.	Blocks	529	20
2.	Panchayats	84787	381
3.	Mukhias	84787	381
4.	Sarpanches	529	20
5.	Pramukhs	529	20
6.	Zila Parishads	1162	51
7.	P.R. Members	11611	523

It was the revolutionary step of the state government for women empowerment. Now women are participating in the decision making processes of the state and a sense of responsibility and self-respect has arisen in the women of Bihar.

Since the PRIs have potential to start the process of women empowerment from the village level, it can change the social scenario of the village. The PRIs provide village women, the opportunities for leadership and to take part directly in the decision making in the process of development. It will also help in managing the violence against women. So the following factors had attracted to take the problem of women empowerment through PRIs for this work. These are:

(a) To create a healthy environment to exercise women's rights equal with men in rural areas.
(b) For equal participation of women in decision making bodies for their development and welfare.
(c) To prepare women for political participation in Parliament and Assemblies also with 33 per cent reservation.
(d) To adopt an integrated approach for empowering women through effective convergence of the services, resources, structures and man power in related sectors.
(e) To organise women into groups as self help groups for economic empowerment of rural areas.
(f) To generate political awareness and political participation in village politics by women through PRIs.

So, the purpose is to search a common platform for political activities of men and women in the grassroots democracy in the district because Samastipur district is a backward district of Bihar in every sphere, economically, educationally and culturally. So, it cannot be expected that gender equality will be maintained. There is a wide gap between the progress and development of men and women in the district and women are not independent in decision making processes, even in domestic affairs due to lack of proper education and training. It can be changed by greater political participation, which is not possible without reservation.

In sample Panchayats, village Rahua, Gohi in Warisnagar block; Janardunpur, Bashudevpur, Jitwaria of Kalyanpur block; Kamla, Malti, Belari of Ujiarpur block; Nagargama, Garsisai of Dalsingsarai block; Mahmmada, Dighra, Kuwauli of Pusa block; Narhan, Samartha in Bibhutipur block and many other panchyats were surveyed and more than two fifties of their population was found illiterate. Especially the condition of female education in the district is not up to the mark. The literary rate in rural area of this district is 44.55 per cent, according to the census of 2001 and among them only 31.16 per cent women are literate. The condition of higher education is also very alarming with the exception of four or five women in each of the village, who have studied beyond middle school level. In Punas village of Samastipur block there is not a single school for girls and there are many examples found during survey that girl students have to go in other villages for schooling. It is largely the men who have studied beyond the high school levels and also acquired jobs outside their respective villages. Lack of education among most of the adult women compelled them to work at home and form as unpaid servants or as hired casual agricultural labours.

So far as the benefits derived from government programmes implemented in these villages during the last ten years are concerned it can be said that the women, especially the poor and dalits, are not getting their proper share in welfare programmes by the officials, mukhias and sarpanches. They are denied their actual benefits like Indira Awas Yojana, Anpurna Yojana, Jawahar Yojana, Red and Green Card Yojana and many beneficial planning related to women and children. Those women, who are influensive and relative of dominant persons, are getting the benefits of these plans in the name of poor and downtrodden women. In most of the villages scheduled castes, landless agricultural labours were not benefited by these schemes. Though government has opened many women and children's welfare centres but facilities for general women are always lacking in these fields also. The noon meal scheme has also become the den of corruption. Though government wants to employ two to three cooks from lower and scheduled caste women from the village to give them employment but it is also not implemented properly in most of the villages.

It is also the fact that most of the government schemes are meant for scheduled caste women, landless and agricultural labours. But it is very pitiable to note that the poor women belonging to backward and upper classes could not secure most of the benefits from the governmental schemes. A balance society must need equality between all inhabitants of the society.

There is an increasing demand that women should be treated on an equal footing with men. They should be given equal opportunities and equal status in possession of various resources such as personal health, assets, land, skills, education, information, knowledge, social status, leadership etc.

Though our Constitution has provided many benefits and schemes for women development and empowerment. Articles 14, 19, 22, 29, 34 to 41, 51 etc. among them in which safeguards are permitted to them by giving right to equality, right to freedom, education, wealth, religious rights etc. but through these safeguards little else have changed. There are no alterations in social institution, in division of labour and the existing power structures. Not only in the district like Samastipur but in whole of India also. The capacities and potentials of women need to be properly tapped, women should be seen not an 'outside the model' but should be considered as an integral part of development. Because the welfare state should not be just a set of services, it has also to be a set of ideas about society, about family and women who have centrally important role to play in it.

The status of women in a society are the true index of its cultural, social and political levels. It is correlated to the participating rights and obligations of women in managing the society and it can be understood with the help of different approaches like.

(a) Demographical indicators
(b) Level of political participation
(c) Impact of developmental programmes
(d) Directly confronting the issues of women

The indifferent attitude of different political parties is also responsible for women's less political awareness. The absence of an active women's movement and the failure of political organisations to mobilize women for political affairs is also considered responsible for less political participation of women.

Increasing violence in the present society has also inspired women for not contesting election and participation. Today election has become a den of criminals, money, men and muscle power which play vital role in elections. Therefore, women want to keep themselves away from this criminal game. Findings show that the women involved in politics mostly come from the economic and political elites of the area. Most of women are not economically strong and election became expensive, therefore, they avoid elections. The sexual abuse and fear of character assassination also hampers women's participation in politics.

In spite of the above mentioned factors, traditional customs and convensions are also responsible for their less participation in politics. Caste system, religious rituals, feudal attitude and family status etc. are among them.

The above approaches not only reflect the status of women in a society but also suggest strategies to empower women. Because empowered women can enjoy their different rights with self-confidence and pride. Empowerment as a concept was introduced at the International Women's Conference in 1985 at Nairobi. Now this concept has rooted in the women's movement throughout the world. The Nairobi International Conference of Women had defined empowerment as redistribution of social power and control of resources in favour of women. In India Sixth Five Year Plan may be called the land-mark for the cause of women's empowerment. The year 2001 had been declared as the year of women empowerment. Ensuring gender equality by removing gender discrimination is the key to real empowerment. For enhancing the status and sustainable achievements in women's empowerment the government of India is developing different programmes and policies as individualistic and collectivistic. Empowerment through awareness building, capacity building and organising women leads to transformation of unequal relationship, increases decision making power in home and community and ensure participation in politics. In this respect women development can be viewed in terms of five hierarchical levels of equality. It can be understood by following chart:

Ability

Women able to make decision

Participation

Organising themselves with men's equality

Conscientisation

Take suitable action to remove gender gaps

Access

Involves equality of access to resources

Welfare

Addresses the basic needs of women

According to Longue, women can reach the status of empowerment through these five stairs.

Thus women form the disadvantaged group in India especially in rural areas. There are various factors responsible for the fact, they are:

(a) The urban middle class bias among the planners, academics, political parties and trade unions alike.
(b) Ignorance of the diversity and plurality that characterised women's role.
(c) Problems and priorities across classes, communities and religion.
(d) Influence of theories of social changes and development and intellectual tools borrowed from West, which are inappropriate for an understanding of a complex society like India.
(e) Failure of women's movement to articulate the problems of all classes of women.

So there is a need of implementing drastic measures to improve women's position especially rural women's position in India. PRIs are the local institutions of administration. There is a need of involving women in playing a significant role in the affairs of the local administration. Because male are not very particularly interested in solving the problem of women like dowry, violence, atrocities on women etc. It is understood that women representatives can play a major role in solving these problems.

Samastipur is a district of Bihar with 20 Blocks, 381 Panchayats and 1250 Villages with semi-urban culture. The following chart can produce the geographical and demographical picture of the district.

Profile of Samastipur District

1.	Establishment year	14.11.1972
2.	Area	2904 sq. km.
3.	Population	3413413
4.	Villages	1250
5.	Panchayats	381
6.	Sex Ratio	F 491 M 509
7.	Total literacy rate	1243542 (45.76%)
	Male	827293 (57.83%)
	Female	436249 (36.21%)
8.	Parliamentary Seats	02
9.	Legislative Seats	10
10.	Zila Parishad Seats	51
11.	Panchayat Samiti Seats	523
12.	Mukhias	381
13.	Sarpanches	381
14.	Pramukhs	20
15.	Ward members	5210

The sex ratio and literacy rate show the poor empowerment condition of women in this district. Since independence, there is not a single woman Member of Parliament had won, it is same with the legislative assembly seats, where a few women participated in election and won. Recently, out of ten seats in Vidhan Sabha only one seat is occupied by a woman. Different political parties are also reluctant to give tickets to women. So before the enforcement

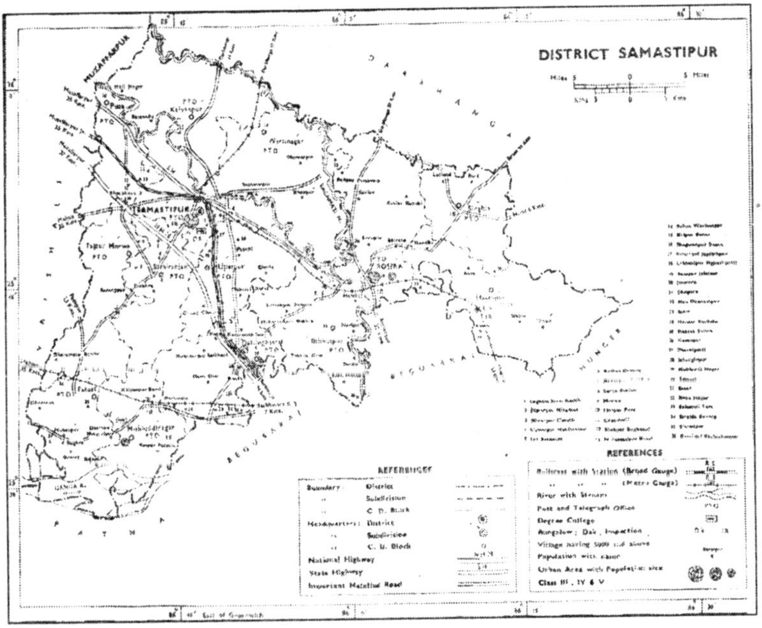

of 73rd Amendment Act, women of this district were not politically empowered. Now after enactment of this Act a drastic change is seen in the rural political atmosphere with fifty per cent reservation for women. Women from different castes and groups now participating in the decision making process of the villages and empowering themselves. So the objectives and purpose of this study is to judge the achievement of 73rd Constitutional Amendment Act in the empowerment and political awareness of women in this district. Through PRIs large number of women's entry into the village political system would ensure changes in the political atmosphere of the villages, the familiar and social perceptions of the role of women and development of grassroots leadership in women. At Gram Sabha and Panchayats level, a new type of leadership would emerge from women entry into these institutions, which is expected to administer better financial resources and would provide constructive thinking in village administration and development. It is the need of the hour. A country like India with village base cannot ignore its 48.9 per cent population, for its proper growth and development.

Need for the Study

There is little concentration among the academic circles to study the problems related to women in present circumstances. Especially in the Panchayati Raj System, women constitute an integral part of our social economic life and actively participate in socio-economic development of the nation. Many works and studies had been conducted on the status and empowerment of women. But due to complex social and cultural processes, illiteracy, poverty, inherent impediments, male dominance in society, the work had been done is not satisfactory, especially for the rural environment of women. Here work of Smt. Niraj Gopal, Department of Political Science of J.N.U., New Delhi, can be cited for its outstanding capacity on women in Panchayati Raj. She had not only mentioned the women's attitude and problems in PRIs but also described society's attitude towards them. She emphasised on the fact that husbands and other family members are the main decision makers and generally discharge the functions of the office of panchayats. The recent study in Meerut says that Pradhanis never attended any meeting or made any decision about allocation of funds to various individuals. They merely sign on the papers. On 17 August 1999, a woman sarpanch was beaten up by extremists at Laxshmidupet in Warangal district of Andhra Pradesh, because she made a statement on village affairs without the consent of her male associates. Though some renowned writers and social status like Prof. Intaz Ahmad, B.R. Nanda, Aruna Asry Alic, C. Gopalan, Smt. Phulrenu Guha, Dr. Vina Majumdar, etc. have worked for the various problems of women. The Government of India and non-governmental organisations are holding national and international seminars, conferences on women study and problems, women's study centres are opened in almost all the major cities of India, works and projects are going on for the development and empowerment of women. Women's study centre at Bhopal and Hyderabad are specially working seriously for the empowerment of women. In 2003 a seminar was organized by the Institute of Objective Studies, New Delhi, on the empowerment of women. Research works and projects are being sponsored by different agencies. Mr. G. Palanithurai of Tamil Nadu in his research paper 'The Genre of Women Leaders in Local Bodies' mentioned the problems and hurdles that a woman representative has to face in performing her day-to-day activity. In the *Indian Journal of Public Administration* Vol. XLVII January-March 2000, he had accepted that though PRIs had given decision making power and empowerment to women but due to male dominance in society, they have to face a lot of difficulty and they have to prove more careful and dutiful to themselves. In the same way Report on Empowerment of Panchayati Raj Institutions on issues related to Population, Health and Social Development sponsored by Population Foundation of India—Rajiv Gandhi Chair for Panchayati Raj Studies 1998: Women's Participation in Panchayati Raj—A Case Study from Tamil Nadu sponsored by Women Commission, M.S. Swaminathan Research Foundation, Chennai, 1999; Promila Dandavate's report on Women's Reservation Bill; magazine, *Rashtra Mahila* Vol. 3, October 1999 Women participation in politics. Hard choices workshop by Research Centre for Women's Studies, S.N.D.T. University, 1991 project work from I.C.S.S.R. on Participation of Women in PRIs System by Dr. G.S. Mehta etc. are the various works for women's empowerment in different areas of women development present the fact that in spite of their effectiveness and efficiency to work they are not treated equal to men in the process of political development. Mrs. Niraj Gopal of J.N.U., New Delhi had clearly mentioned after research that husbands are always there first working for the election of their wives and then goading from behind for their success. She had cited plenty of examples of surrogate and proxy representation of husbands and other male relatives, who not only canvas for their women candidates but also receive notices and attending meetings on their behalf.

Various research studies have been conducted to study the women leadership at panchayat level in different states. The women's representation has been very encouraging in states like West Bengal, Haryana, Maharashtra, and Rajasthan. In Kerala and Karnataka, in Gram Panchayat elections, not only

33 per cent but over 43 per cent seats have been captured by women. In recent election of 2006 in Bihar, the present Chief Minister Mr. Nitish Kumar had reserved 50 per cent seats for women in PRIs and urban local body institutions and about 64 per cent seats in both elections are occupied by women. In such a backward state like Bihar this charisma had occurred due to 50 per cent reservation, which had awakened the society and women. Even in the state of Orissa a large number of women have come to power at grassroots level. This achievement becomes all the more spectacular when it is seen against the backdrop of a low literacy level of women in the state, which is 29.1 per cent only. So the outcome of these studies is of mixed nature.

The studies in different states reflect that women were used as proxies. The proxies suffer from certain characteristics:

(a) They display a lower level of political awareness.
(b) They show their primary loyalty to their family.
(c) Their role as an elected representative is merely an extension of their role as a housewife.
(d) They serve the paternal interests of the family.
(e) They enter in politics to save the constituency for their male relatives.

Above mentioned facts are responsible for renewal of the study regarding women's political empowerment through PRIs, especially in the rural areas like Samastipur district of Bihar. Samastipur district is among the most backward districts of Bihar—culturally, educationally and politically. Women constitute nearly 48.1 per cent of population in the district but their political empowerment was below the mark before 73rd and 74th Constitutional Amendment Acts. And this political awareness of women also does not differ significantly between urban and rural areas. On the whole working women including professionals have greater awareness but this is not always reflected in participation. In Indian democracy election has become a game of families. It is related to ten thousand renowned families, there is no question who wins and which party wins, power revolves among the members of these families. So there is not any possibility of any link between higher socio-economic status and political awareness. Some of the studies initiated that political awareness is less among women in the higher income groups, who have a negligible interest in politics, though many of the women legislators come from rich and well to do families. It is also found in observation that the difference in the level of political information and understanding between men and women are still continued.

The indifferent attitude of political parties is also responsible for this cause. No political party wants participation of women as candidate in election. Though they honour women but very few are in favour of women's active participation in election as candidate. This is the fact that women Representation Bill is still pending in the parliament. No party is willing to give 33 per cent reservation to women in election, but does not want to be exposed. During elections, when women voters are taken seriously for vote purpose women's participation in political process is a must for today's political atmosphere because of the following factors:-

(a) Success of the democracy demands full participation of all its able citizens. Women form half of its citizens and any negligence of women representative is the negligence of half population of the country.
(b) Political participation of women helps in measuring their degree of political awareness and choices.
(c) Women are the active agents of socio-economic transformation in rural areas. They have the potentials for effective working and pooling of resources. They can understand better, problems, identify them, give priorities and preferences and are aware of strategies towards the solution. Hence their active participation will not only enhance the status of women in the villages but will also help in development of the villages.
(e) To initiate, formulate and implement policies and programmes which will benefit women. It has been observed that in most of the panchayats the decision making has been in favour of men, and the needs of rural women go unnoticed.

(f) To bring in a feminine perspective to the process of planning, policy formulation and execution of rural development programmes. It is expected that more women would change the focus of rural administration towards important facts of life like health, nutrition, child-welfare schemes, family care schemes, drinking water facilities etc.

(g) Representation of more women in village panchayats would play a major role to empower women. Empowering women refers to strengthening their innate capacities through acquiring knowledge, power and experience.

(h) The elected women can act as an intermediary between the government and the women in rural areas. Their accessibility to other women in the village, their contacts at the grassroots and their awareness of the needs and interest of women will improve the condition of women in rural areas.

(i) It will provide a platform for women to gain experience to overcome their fear and built in confidence break the walls of patriarchy and orthodoxy. It will create an access to women at state and national level politics.

(j) Larger participation will provide women an exposure to outside world. Their participation would improve their status in society as well as in their home. It would also give them an opportunity to work in groups on projects of common interest.

There are the various reasons that the study of the impact of PRIs on women's political role is essential. Because Panchayati Raj Institutions have always considered as a means of good governance. It is associated with effective and efficient administration in a democratic framework. India is a country of villages. About 80 per cent of its population live in villages and true good governance can be achieved by the all-round development of villages. Mahatma Gandhi had also accepted "India's independence must begin at the bottom". Panchayati Raj as a system of governance at the grassroots level in rural

India has rightly conceived as the most viable and proper mechanism of realising the goals of democracy. And through 50 per cent reservation in PRIs in Bihar the goal of 'Purna Swaraj' of Mahatma Gandhi can be achieved no doubt.

Role of women in PRIs and empowerment of women through PRIs is a vital issue today but none of the socialist or political scientist had taken the issue seriously. A National conference of three days sponsored by UGC and ICSSR was organised in the Department of Political Science, R.N.A.R. College, Samastipur, Bihar in October 2006 on the topic 'Role and Relevance of Local Self-Government on Democracy' under the convenorship of Dr. Minni Thakur, Head of Department, Political Science in which nearly 200 participants from different parts of the country presented their papers and discussed the various aspects of PRIs, especially on participation of women and weaker section and the impact of PRI on them.

So this study is an attempt to understand the role played by women in political arena of the region of Samastipur district. It is observed that there are inter-villages and panchyats variations in the position and role of the women. Various factors such as caste, class, creed, customs, religion, cultural millieu etc. play crucial role in determinant of the position of women in this district. Has the Samastipur district progressed in these terms and to what extent women are benefited by this progress? What role they ascribe for themselves and are they able to play effective role at different levels and actively participate in different spheres of life? These are the important questions form the major concern of this study.

Women are supposed to be the targets for development. There is a need to look at them as important participants also. So the status of women in a society can be judged by many factors—demographic indicators, their political participation, impact of different developmental programmes on their status. This study will certainly try to find out an amicable settlement for all the questions and will be an asset for the women's study in rural areas also. Because there is a need of implementing drastic measures to improve women's position in India. There is a need of involving women in playing a significant role in the affairs of the state. They should participate in decision making and contribution to solve the problems of national development. Such study will help in comparative evolution and building up strategies for increasing participation of women. So the present study looks at women's participation through the case study of Samastipur district of Bihar.

Utility and Objective of the Study

Women are the half population of the country. Any development and progress of the country depends upon the development and progress of the whole society. Therefore, the principles of gender equality and equity and protection of women's right has been the prime concern of thinkers from the very day of independence. Accordingly, the countries concern in safeguarding the rights and privileges of women found its best expression in the contribution of India while Article 14 of the Constitution confers equal opportunities for men and women in political, social and economic fields. Article 15 prohibits discrimination against any citizen on the ground of sex, religion, race, caste etc. And there are so many Articles related to social justice and women safeguard. But nothing had been done in this field, especially in rural areas.

The place of Indian rural women in social, economic and political spheres is more depress than urban counterparts. Although the rural women have been contributing significantly in the social and economic progress of the country, their participation in development programmes has not been appreciated. In political aspects, they remain largely inactive and indifferent due to various socio-economic constraints and also due to the absence of serious political and social motivation. Political participation of rural women as person holding high office in political organisations, as candidates for some elective positions, campaigners except as voters has been very negligible. This is the reason that rural women remain aloof from the political and developmental processes.

It has been realised that unless rural women are involved in the developmental process, the overall socio-economic development of the country cannot be fully gained.

To study the status of women in the changing society and

changing rural environment is the need of today's social inquiry. Dream of social justice, Ram Rajya and social reconstruction cannot be achieved unless and until the problems of rural women are studied.

There are limited research studies on the problems of rural women. There are also a lack of studies, which can cover the various social and political legislation and organisation, which have profound influence on the development of rural women in Bihar. Because data on rural women in different spheres are very much needed by planners, administrators and social workers for identifying the problems of rural women and to find out correct and proper remedies for it.

Rural women of Bihar are just living as a second class citizen in society. The tale of female harassment begins from her mother's womb and continues till she died. A large number of Indian women are subjected to discrimination, oppression and exploitation. It is within the family and society also. In our patriarchal society the secondary status and role of women is mainly responsible for the physical, mental and social atrocities of women. The practice of female foeticide female infanticide, the practice of bride burning for dowry, cases of rape and suicide are some of the examples of oppression and exploitation. The position of widow or single woman is also very pathetic. Speaking at the conference on women Mrs. Margaret Alva accepted that in spite of increasing awareness among women about their rights, all social indicators present a dismal picture of their position. Robbed of dignity, pride and self-worth women see themselves as prisoners or slaves doomed to obedience and conformity. And it is the truth that maximum Indian women find release and freedom only in dead.

The all India crime rate reported to the police were estimated 12.4 per cent at the national level. It has been observed that large percentage of crime against women goes unreported due to social stigma attached to them. The following Table shows the reported crime list on women in India in different years.

This list is not adequate because large number of cases are unreported due to prestige and pride.

Table 1.3: Increase of crimes in India

Crime	*Year*			*Rate of increase*
	1996	*1997*	*1998*	
Atrocities	14846	15330	15031	2.0
Kidnapping	14877	15617	16381	4.9
Dowry death	5513	6006	6917	15.2
Torture	35246	36592	41318	12.9
Suicides	28939	30764	31046	0.9
Sexual harassment	5671	5796	8123	40.1
Shifting of girls	182	78	146	87.2
Sati	0	01	0	100.0
Shifting of women	7706	8323	8695	4.5
Painting of women as obscene	96	73	192	16.3
Dory related Dowry	2647	2685	3489	29.9
Rape	1209	1318	1305	—

In spite of the division of the Bihar, state is the third most populous state in India after Uttar Pradesh and Maharashtra. The sex ratio of the state according to 2001 census and National Survey Commission is 921 females per 1000 males. Darbhanga and Samsatipur districts have also been declining sex ratio of 914 and 917 respectively. There are many social obstacles which resist the progress and development of women in their region.

Rural Bihar, especially Mithila region is the most neglected part of the country. The socio-economic condition of the region is not upto the mark due to natural calamities like flood, excess rain, irregular and partial employment which forced the men labourers to migrate to other states. A large number of male members from almost every family use to go Punjab, Haryana, and Kolkata for wage earning and employment. It is natural that the whole burden of the family including children and old men, transferred to women. Therefore, political empowerment is very important for the women of this region. The political participation in all stages and all activities was very poor in women of this region before 73rd Amendment Act. Only 4.2 per cent of women were involved in different political activities. The 73rd Amendment to the Constitution passed by the parliament and adopted by the states in 1993 provided for one-third reservation of seats for women in local body institutions. In 2006 election of Panchayati Raj Institutions, it was enhanced 50 per cent for women. This has been hailed as a great achievement in the empowerment of women and around one million women have come to power in decision making process through this legislation at the panchyat level. Now almost a million women occupy positions as members and chairpersons in the three tier structure introduced by this amendment in India.

But there are so many questions arise on the real functioning and outcomings of this legislation. It may be asked that are women really empowered through this Act?

No doubt, this amendment had given specific and broad powers to women members but there is certain impediment in the way of fruitful results. They are not free in decision making at any stage, rather their male relatives perform their whole work. Most of the lady members at the time of observation accepted that they often attend meetings and take decision because of the ignorance of the subject, and male dominance in the family. *Purda Pratha* also makes them away from fieldworks and participation in meetings. When these members hail from well to do political families, they have less problem, they often go to meetings and field observations. They also take part in discussion and debates. But the women representatives of middle class and scheduled caste have to face many difficulties. The official did not cooperate them. They always try to misguide them on any issue. Because most of the panchayat and zila parishad members are uneducated and illiterate, they have no clear vision of administration. Samastipur district of Bihar is dominated by Koeri, Yadav and Dusadh castes. Bhumihar is also an important caste in decision making process but its number comes 8th or 9th in domination. Pusa block, Kalyanpur block etc. have maximum Bhumihar population but they are not united in political arrangement, this is the reason that out of 10 Legislative Assembly seats, most are represented by Koeri-caste and in two MP seats, one by Koeri and other by Dusadh caste. In this district Koeri caste is famous for their notorious and criminal affairs. After reservation women of all castes are benefited and got their place in political processes.

So, many works are done on women problems, but what problem a rural woman has to face in her day-to-day activity and how does she manage her skill in solving her problem, how society and environment react on women's behaviour and how much they are empowered in solving their problem through the reservation in Constitutional Amendment Act 1992 are the main thrust area of the research. For this purpose a questionnaire is prepared with these problems and circulated within panchayats of sample block. Interviews and group discussions were also organised by the researcher for amicable solution. It will also guide the coming generation of women to make active participation in assembly and parliament elections. Because in the process of observation one Sumitra Devi of Kalonzer village of Kalyanpur block had presented her view that if Rabrī Devi, an illiterate woman, has been controling the state for nine years, while not we should also do something for our village? So a scene of consciousness is awakening in rural women regarding their rights and duties towards society.

The main aim and objective of this minor project work is to attract the attention of the society in general and government in particular to the problems of the women, their political unknownness and the role of the Panchayati Raj Institution in support of their political empowerment. So the major objective of this project is as follows:

1. To review the existing literature on women in politics in general.
2. To study in detail and analyse the Panchayati Raj System and participation of women in the wake of 73rd Constitutional Act.
3. To study the socio-economic and political profile of rural women.
4. To study the political awareness of women in rural areas through 73rd Amendment Act.
5. To analyse the nature and extent of political linkage of women Panchayati Raj leaders.
6. To study the views and observations of women

representatives on various aspects of PRIs and rural development.
7. To examine the problem of finance of the Panchayati Raj Institutions for implementation of various schemes.
8. To study the view of society about women after 73rd Amendment Act.
9. To study the impact of 73rd Amendment Act on the political participation and awakenness of women.
10. To study the fact that Panchayati Raj Institutions are really a road way for women empowerment.
11. To suggest remedies of the identified problems in the region.

For the fruitful progress of women's study, many government and non-government agencies are working. The international year for women and the publication of the report on status of women in India (1974) gave a new turn to women studies in India. Many research centres including literacy analysis, development policies, education, health, political process, violence and crime are established. Many seminars, symposiums, and conferences are organising everywhere in India but there is a lack of full length work on women and Panchayati Raj especially of rural women and Panchayati Raj and of rural women in Mithila Region. The present study will be a full-fledged study, focusing on various aspects, problems of women and their solution by Panchayati Raj Institutions. No doubt, it will be helpful for the women of the district and for government also to implement necessary solutions of their problems.

Methodology

The study is based on survey research methodology. This is an exploratory and diagnostic research design based on two types of data (a) primary data and (b) secondary data.

The primary data were collected from different panchayats of ten blocks—Samastipur, Pusa, Kalyanpur, Sarairanjan, Patori, Ujiarpur, Dalsingsarai, Vidyapatinagar, Vibhutipur and Warisnagar of Samastipur district through questionnaire and interview method. Since women respondents form the primary source of information, a comprehensive interview schedule was prepared. In the same way a questionnaire with all necessary information was prepared and distributed among respondents of these at random chosen panchayats. Observation method was also used during the data collection. So it may be said that in this study, we have used two main sociological methods—interview and observation. The secondary data is collected from the books, journals, magazines, newspapers, works done by voluntary organisations, the census reports of 1991, 2001, Government survey and collectorate and block offices in the district.

Interview

A questionnaire regarding political awareness and empowerment of women was prepared for interview. The respondents have to give information about their personal profile also regarding age, caste, education, sex, family status etc. Then question regarding political consciousness and empowerment is asked by them by the assistant of the investigator. The interview was conducted in person with assistant in each sample block of the district with panchayat also. Male, female with PRI representatives and general people were interviewed at random basis. There was no difference made on the ground of caste, sex, age or group in the interview. Any member or inhabitant of the sampling panchayat willing to interview was given the chance. In the same way a well designed questionnaire was framed to collect the primary data. The questionnaire was distributed among ten to fifteen persons, male and female, in sample panchayats for data collection. Over two hundred females and fifty males were interviewed through this process. The following process was adopted for data collection.

A. Classification of Respondents

In our survey total 250 female and male respondents were selected at random basis from the different panchayats of the sampling block. Out of 250, 105 respondents were of general categories, 95 were from backward classes and 50 were from scheduled castes. There were no respondents from scheduled tribes and others.

Table 1.4: Castewise distribution of the respondents

GC	BC	SC	ST	Others	Total
105	95	50	X	X	250

Table 1.5: Agewise distribution of the respondents

Sex	25-35	35-45	45-60	60 and above	Total
F	92	75	33	nil	200
M	18	24	06	02	50

Out of 200 female respondents 92 were of the age group of twenty-five to thirty-five years. Then 75 were of thirty-five to forty-three years of age. In the age group of forty-five to sixty-only thirty-five women were participated and in the age of sixty and above no respondent was found. But maximum number of this age group was also in favour of women's participation in politics. Smt. Budhia Devi, age sixty-two years from Malinagar panchayat of Pusa block resisted because she had grievances from the local politicians and she felt politics, a waste of time and money, otherwise maximum women were in favour of political participation.

Table 1.6: Educational qualification of the respondents

Sex	Nil	Below 6	Below 10	Below Inter	BA	Total
F	33	58	85	21	03	200
M	02	08	20	08	12	50

In educational background these sampling blocks were not up to the mark. Especially, those panchayat members and Zila Parishad members who belong to 25 to 35 years of age, had low level of education. There are many Mukhias and Sarpanches who were illiterate and unknown from the mode of local politics. Mukhia of Mathurapur Panchayat of

Warisnagar block Smt. Renu Devi (Sah) is totally illiterate in the same way Banarsi Devi Mukhia of Janardanpur Panchayat is also illiterate. In Zila Parishad also out of 24 members in the sampling blocks 16 are illiterate. It is just reverse in male members because maximum Panchayati Raj male members are literate and have knowledge of politics.

Table 1.7: Income of the respondents

Sex	*Nil*	*Low*	*Agri.*	*Service*	*High*	*Total*
F	100	38	32	12	18	200
M	Nil	10	26	08	06	50

It is the general survey and interview of random sampling panchayats. A set of questionnaire has been prepared to interview the Panchayati Raj members about their thinking and ideas of participation and political consciousness. For example, some of the questions and responses are given below for observation:

B. 1. Did you feel empowered with PRIs Constitutional Amendment Act, 1992?

Table 1.8

Post	*Yes*	*No*	*Don't Know*	*Precentage*
Zila Parishad	35	07	08	50
Mukhia	15	23	12	50
Panch members	10	28	12	50

2. Do you represent the village problem directly or some one else on behalf of you?

Table 1.9

Post	*Myself*	*Family*	*Others*	*Total*
Zila Parishad	06	20	24	50
Mukhia	08	18	24	50
Sarpanch	04	25	21	50
Panch members	02	30	18	50

3. Did you follow the discussion and involve in it?

Table 1.10

Group	*No*	*Little*	*Yes*	*Well versed*
F	05	29	10	06
M	Nil	09	22	19

4. Has reservation enhanced the capacity of political participation of women?

Table 1.11

Group	*No*	*Little*	*Yes*	*Total*
F	10	05	35	50
M	08	10	32	50

5. Did you think that customs and traditions are the main obstacles in the progress of society and nation?

Table 1.12

Group	*No*	*Yes*	*Little*	*Absolutely*	*Total*
F	25	05	09	09	50
M	20	10	08	12	50

6. Do you take your own decision or guided by someone else?

Table 1.13

Post	*Myself*	*Family*	*Other*	*Total*
Zila Parishad	10	22	18	50
Mukhia	09	17	24	50
Sarpanch	05	24	21	50
Panch Members	04	30	16	50

7. Do you think that in a changing society role of women in all aspects is important?

Table 1.14

Post	No	Little	Yes	Absolute	Total
Zila Parishad	12	08	18	12	50
Mukhia	08	10	12	20	50
Sarpanch	10	22	08	10	50
Panch members	16	14	12	08	50

8. Do you think that women PRI members can stop corruption?

Table 1.15

Post	No	Little	Yes	Absolute	Total
Zila Parishad	10	12	15	13	50
Mukhia	15	12	13	10	50
Sarpanch	13	17	12	08	50
Panch members	21	12	11	06	50

9. Do you think that through the process of PRIs dream of democracy can be achieved?

Table 1.16

Post	No	Little	Yes	Absolute	Total
Zila Parishad	03	10	20	17	50
Mukhia	06	10	12	22	50
Sarpanch	10	12	15	13	50
Panch members	10	10	17	13	50

10. Do you think that reservation for women in PRIs is a wise decision?

Table 1.17

Post	No	Little	Yes	Absolute	Total
Zila Parishad	04	06	25	15	50
Mukhia	08	10	22	10	50
Sarpanch	09	11	20	10	50
Panch members	10	15	15	10	50

11. Do you think that reservation for women should be extended to parliament and state assemblies?

Table 1.18

Post	*No*	*Little*	*Yes*	*Absolute*	*Total*
Zila Parishad	04	06	30	10	50
Mukhia	03	05	20	22	50
Sarpanch	06	08	25	10	50
Panch members	08	08	24	10	50

There is a lot of changes in the statement of different PRI members. At the time of election out of 50 female PRI members (Mukhias, Zila Praishads, Sarpanches etc.) answered that they were not involved in the discussion in the panchayat meetings. But after two years of stay in office most of them accepted that they are actively taking part in the proceedings of the meetings. In answer to the family involvement and their role, most of the women had accepted that due to the engagement in meeting and offices their family had been neglected, especially their children and old members of the family. Because most of the respondents of PRIs were at the age group between 25 and 40 having small children and joint families. Out of 50 respondents 15 had accepted that their main source of income is agriculture and after being members their agriculture work was hampered due to lack of time and 18 of them answered that their husbands and in-laws were not happy with their involvement in Panchayati Raj Institution. Among 50 participants, 42 answered that they were not happy with their officials. Because they did not cooperate them in decision making process. Most of them complained that those officials tried to keep them in dark in vital issues of development and even issues of women's and child development were also kept away from these lady PRI members. In observation the system is found common in scheduled caste lady members also. In the same way most of the lady participants had accepted that maximum decision in the meeting were completed by their male partners. Some backward caste women in Zhauri Panchayat of Birsingpur village of Kalyanpur block had complained that mukhia Smt.

Chanchala Devi always ignored the interest of poor and down troddens and she hardly took any decision herself. Her husband and family members take decision on behalf of her. So this type of incident found common in the sampling panchayats.

So it may be concluded that through interviews and group discussion with a set of questionnaire, it is found that most of the PRI members had politically awakened. They are struggling for their rights and proper place in the society. There is very need and necessity to encourage them to improve their skill and efficiency. To make them more efficient and perfect, proper orientation and training should be arranged for them in dealing with the public and for better adjustment with society.

Observation and Field Study

The study has attempted to understand the political participation and role of women through Panchayati Raj Institutions in Samastipur district. The three major objectives are:

1. To understand the role played by women at various levels in the political processes of the Samastipur district as participants, grassroots leaders and activists.
2. To look after the impact and significance of such participation, women's right and living condition.
3. To assess the role played by the 73rd Constitutional Amendment Act to promote women's political awareness.

The study has exposed a large number of paradoxes existing in the districts, sample villages and panchayats. The spell of fieldwork was not totally satisfactory and the investigator had to face pleasant and unpleasant both situations at the time of interview and discussions. Maximum of women especially agricultural labourers were not able to appreciate or understand the value of such research, therefore hesitating to answer the questions. For example, when the investigator went to Srirampur village of Pusa block in a Dalit Basti one Munia Devi with a dozen women came forward with curiosity about the entrant in village but when they came to know that they wanted to know something from them, they left the place and went to their fields or home. One Shabo Devi answered questions related to her but when we came on her husband and family members she refused to answer the questions. The same situation was faced in at least 20 villages of different panchayats in the sampling blocks. But there are women like Bimla Devi, a master-degree holder in Home Science in Kalonzer panchayat in Samastipur, Bihar, she not only cooperated us whole heartedly, but also convinced other women for the purpose of the interview. It is due to the variation in the culture of this Semi Urban district which combines a synthesis of traditional and modern values of society. It has assimilated elements of various customs, backward and forward castes with Muslim population and has pervasive influence of Mithila culture. All classes and castes of people are influenced by Mithila tradition, culture and customs like Madhusharamni, Kojagra, Duragwan, Nagpanchami, Gauri Pujan are adopted by all castes and classes of this region. In Mithila culture Kumari Pujan is an important part of every ritual, which is seen common in the whole district. There is a great adoration for Bhagwati in this area and people of this region celebrate Navratra with great enthusism. In the poetries of Vidyapati, this culture of Mithila can be seen.

The forces of modernization, progress and development influence the region. This has resulted in better prospects for women in the district. There are paradoxes which were seen while trying to understand the women political participation and role in the district.

Samastipur district is a combination of 20 blocks with 1250 villages and 381panchayats covering 3413413 population in itself. It has semi-urban culture so reflection of urbanisation has been seen in the culture of the villages also. Villages are hardly 20 to 25 km away from the headquarter. Blocks like Pusa, Kalyanpur, Tajpur, have adopted the culture of Muzaffarpur district while Warisnagar, Khanpur, etc. adopted Darbhanga culture in the same way blocks like Bibhutipur, Ujiarpur, Dalsingsarai etc. have adopted the mixed culture of Begusarai and Darbhanga districts.

Women constitute 46.3 per cent of population but the position of women in Samastipur district is not very satisfactory. The position of women can be assessed from the social, educational, cultural and political parameters of any society, their equality with men. It is markable that it is the land of Pandit Mandan Mishra whose wife Bharti had defeated Shankracharya in the religious discourse, who was famous for her knowledge and wit. It is also true that in the war of independence, women of this district participated fearlessly under the leadership of Mahatma Gandhi. But after independence the status of women declined everywhere and the district is not remained untouched. Though women receive better treatment in society but their position in family is not satisfactory due to heavy dowry system, inequality between male and female child, male dominance in family and society etc. Economically 71.2 per cent women depend on their family and only 22.8 per cent are engaged in any job. This is due to reservation in different jobs for women by the recent government of Mr. Nitish Kumar, they are engaged in Shiksha Mitra, Nyaya Mitra, Anganwari Sewika, Asha Bahu in blocks but only 2-3 per cent of higher posts are occupied by the women, which is very low for the progress of the district. The education rate of girl child is also not up to the mark. Only 32.8 per cent women are educated in the district. Though government had provided education to girls in every village and panchayats through primary schools but the number of high schools is inadequate in the villages. It is shameful that there are no separate high school for girls in most of these villages. They have to go in other village for higher education and poor farmers and villagers cannot afford such type of education. Therefore, maximum number of girls left the education after completing middle school education.

Samastipur district has 10 MLA seats and 2 MP seats. Since independence till now, only 4 MLAs and not any MP seat is won by women candidates. Ramsukumani Devi of Congress party won the election three times from Kalyanpur seat of Vidhan Sabha and now Smt. Aswamedh Devi of Janata Dal (U) has been elected on the seat for two terms. But none of other constituency, has woman member since independence.

Political parties either of national or regional level are not interested in women's participation as candidates. This is the reason, that women as a voter, participate in large number but as a candidate in general election their participation is very marginal. Aswamedh Devi was given ticket because her husband was killed in a political rivalry and due to sympathy vote, she won the election in the Koeri dominated constituency of Kalyanpur, because she also belonged to the same caste. Caste and situation play vital role in women's political participation, otherwise all parties are reluctant to give ticket to women candidates. The following trend was observed with regard to political participation of women in the district:

> The percentage of women voters has been high and the gender gap in voting turnout is very narrow. Women are enthusiastic about voting. Though percentage of voting had declined when compared with the previous election but the number of women voters had increased. It is also seen in observation that women were not independent voters, especially in middle class families and Muslim families. They were dependent on men in making political decisions. Family is a cohesive unit and both men and women form its major components. The members are likely to act on a united front after mutual discussions and agreements to achieve the best for family.

Before Panchayati Raj Institutions election mostly and after some cases show that women are not also very enthusiastic of entering politics. They think politics as a dirty game with increasing greed, conflicts and unholy competition. So women are less willing to enter into politics, but most of them enter into politics in Panchayati Raj election on the pressure of their family, especially their husbands. They are more interested in solving their day to-day problem. Even in the observation, it was found that educated women had show less interest in political participation.

Most of the women had contested because their male family members were involved in active politics. Now the seat was reserved for women, so it was their fate to contest the seat. But there are also the women found in the observation that they took keen interest in politics, who willingly participated in Panchayati Raj election and won.

Though Panchayati Raj Act had increased the powers of panchayats with 29 vital subjects of development but the elected women have not been able to contribute in any constructive way towards the gender cause. It was felt that women representatives would solve the feministic problems effectively and properly but till now it has not achieved satisfaction. In most of the panchayats child marriage, polygamy, dowry system, atrocities on women, male dominance in family are on increase. Even they are not succeeded in controlling alcoholism in villages which ruins the economic development of the family. The dropout rate from schools of girls is not controlled in schools, though government had made many laws to increase girls education and the panchayats had got adequate power to implement these schemes. But the goal is not achieved by women Panchayati Raj Institution members as it was understood.

One thing is interesting in the observation that women's participation in Panchayati Raj Institution covers all castes. They attained *morcha, rallies, dharna* for common needs. But men are the main movers of the women. They lead the parameter for the struggle and even decided the role to be played by women. The role of women is regarded as supplementary and supportive and it should be performed within the accepted framework, without challenging traditional norms and status. People want conventional role of women and could not accept women competing with men in the power structure.

The studies in different panchayats reflect the fact that women are used as proxies because they display a lower level of political awareness. They owe their primary loyalty to their family and they serve the patriarchal interest of the family. But most important is that they entered the political arena for protecting the constituency of their male relatives.

In the observation, illiteracy is considered as a major cause for women to be used as sheer proxies. It is found that a majority of women panches were housewives and were either uneducated or educated up to primary level. In the large number of cases the decision to participate in the election was not of their own. And it is the male members, who are exercising the power by proxy. The institution of Sarpanchpati and Mukhiapati might not have any legal sanction but it is governing almost all the panchayats of the district. Not only in Samastipur district, but in the whole Bihar. Sarpanchpati and Mukhiapati are working on behalf of their wives in decision making processes. Female illiteracy and lack of independent voting rights did not allow women to play active role in the village politics. Most of the lady mukhias and sarpanches are helpless and not attending meetings regularly.

It was also found that the male member of the family often dominated the panches and other members of the PRIs. Therefore women panches are not interested in contesting the election second time. The Zila Parishad members are also not working satisfactorily. Majority of elected Zila Parishad members had no experience of active politics, usually male members of their family make pressure on them to contest. They are only instrumental and make themselves busy in household activities. Samastipur Zila Parishad had lady chairperson and vice chairperson and are suitable examples of these facts.

Another observation by the study is that unlike the trends at national and state politics, there is predominance of young women in grassroots politics. Women between the age group of 35 to 50 years are active to join grassroots politics in spite of their domestic burdens. The President and Vice President of Zila Parishad are both young women within 45 years of age. In sampling Zila Parishad out of 25, 20 are of the age group of 25 to 40 years.

In Samastipur district, caste plays an important role in elections. Victory of a candidate depends upon the role of caste leaders in the constituency. Dominant personalities of different castes decide the candidate in the election. There are four main castes in the district. They are Koeri, Yadav, Bhumihar and Dusadh. So it seems that all political activities of the region revolves on caste line.

Schedule XI to the Constitutional Amendment Act had given vital subjects for working of Panchayati Raj Institutions. The government had announced that all village planning should be prepared, surveyed and implemented by Panchayati Raj Institutions. So there is competition among people for candidature in these elections.

During survey, interview was conducted for knowing the hurdles and problems of any kind that a woman representative had to face in their day-to-day activity. Lot of problems are found in the survey.

These women representatives have to face a lot of individual and family problems. Women leaders hailing from upper literate class, can tackle the problem of administration to some extent because their education and knowledge. But the dalit and uneducated women are economically and socially not in a position to understand the political activities. They are dependent on their officials and male partners. Lack of managerial skill is also a weakness of the women; they are unable to manage things in favour of themselves. The state of non-payment also made women take themselves out from the politics. The members of Panchayati Raj Institutions did not get any salary or remuneration for their work. It is not possible for women, who are wage earners to work honestly without any remuneration.

The main reason of functional shortcoming may be derived from the fact that in India, democracy is simply a political arrangement for power sharing. A report published in *Economic Times* in April 2002 says a careful analysis of nearly 500 legislative offices in the state and at the centre will reveal that probably two-third of them are controlled by about ten thousand well known families. No matter which party wins power alternates between the members of these families in India. There are 4120 MLA and 841 MP seats in India and reality is that the legislature has become more a disguised and unaccountable executive than people's representatives. It is similar with the Panchayati Raj Institutions. Almost maximum of seats in all categories are captured by the dominated personalities of the area, not through bullet but through ballot.

It has also been found in observation that officials are not cooperating with the female members properly. In Kalyanpur,

Rosera, Patori, Sarairanjan blocks everywhere, these female members had complained the non-cooperation from officials. Even Zila Parishad members had also complained.

The research study conducted on the functioning of Panchayati Raj Institution for women's political participation and effect of the Constitutional Amendment Act 1992 on women's participation and emerging political role of women. Before the enforcement of the Act, there was marginal role of women in the field of local self-government in Samastipur district. But after enactment of the Act their role and participation had increased. They are fifty per cent in number and are gaining political consciousness gradually. Mukhia of Ladaura Panchayat of Kalyanpur block voiced for removal of wine shop from the village and was succeeded. Indu Devi, sarpanch of Darsur panchayat of Warisnagar block had struggled for electric and water supply in her village. Renu Sah mukhia of Mathurapur panchayat of Warisnagar block also battled for better implementation of government scheme for the people for whom it was meant. In Jitwarpur panchayat of Samastipur block panch member Dukhia Devi, Survi Devi, Rama Devi have battled for the atrocities on women of their *Tola*. They also tried to stop alcoholism in the panchayat, though they were not succeeded but they tried their best to remove this evil practice. In Janardanpur panchayat, Bainy panchayat and many other panchayats women members successfully stopped the employers from hiring labour for less than the minimum wages from outside their villages depriving of the women their wages and work. This is not the end, elected members from many panchayats in the district have taken part against wages and drinking water, electric supply. Samastipur district is a flood prone area and these elected members of local bodies also raised their voice for proper and timely relief for flood victims. They got the power of the allotment of houses to them. In the recent flood of 2007 the situation in 12 blocks out of 20 blocks was very alarming. These women representatives worked hard for the safety and proper care of their panchayat people. There are a lot of cases in different blocks where these members had done their best in solving this natural calamity. These women had raised many issues like alcoholism, lotteries, health and sanitation, education benefits, drinking water problem, electrification of villages, atrocities on women etc. It was also seen that members attached with any self help group are more particular to raise the issue related to women's development. Budhia Devi, Sarita Kumari of Nagargama village of Dalsingsarai, Santi Devi of Nagargama sarpanch are working with the support of these self help groups for women's development and economic empowerment. These women in the local bodies have made a difference through their sincere, dedicated and mature steps to the issues affected to the inhabitants of their panchayat in day-to-day activities. During observation one thing was found very touching. Most of the representatives had complained that they were not getting any allowance or salary and they had to spend from their own pocket in making visits or in attending meetings. This factor is also responsible for their aloofness from the active politics. Mukhias have no such type of complaint, because they have many funds. But sarpanches and panch members complained about financial problems.

Though impact of the Constitutional Amendment Act 1992, women's entry into local politics has influenced the quality of their lives. The study looked into following aspects:-

(a) Challenges from the Family
(b) Relief from Domestic Activities
(c) Challenges from male dominated society

(a) Challenges from the Family

Family is an internal part of the society and women play an important role in establishing balance in a family. It is considered that because of the entry into politics, women cannot spend their time in domestic work and family affairs. So it will ruin the peace and harmony of the family. The children, old persons, husbands and their relatives may be ignored due to extra pressure of work on women. Family is regarded as scared institution in India and women have been given greater responsibility of looking after the prospects of the members of a family. This is the very cause that before fifty per cent reservation in Panchayati Raj Institutions women participation was very poor. Samastipur district has 381 panchayats and before 2006 elections of Panchayati Raj there was only one lady Mukhia in Samastipur district. Because mukhia seat was previewed from reservation and the situation of the district was not in favour of women political participation. The Mukhia was chosen not for her ability and administrative knowledge but because she was the wife of a dominating rich man of the area.

But after the enactment of the Act the situation was changed. Fifty per cent reservation had changed the scenario. Now there are 190 out of 381 lady mukhias are working in different panchayats of the district. In the survey in Kalyanpur block in the 31 panchayats there are 15 lady mukhias were elected on reservation. All lady mukhias are married and are of different castes and classes. They have children and most of them are of the age group of 25 to 40 years.

Most of them live in a joint family and all of them come from rural agricultural family. When asked, whether they were able to devote time and attention to their house, all responded in affirmative. Many of them felt that after being elected on the post, their image was highlighted in family and society. Children of these members also realised the dignity of their mother in spite of their domestic image. Though their work load was increased, because they have to attain meetings, visit villages of the panchayat, meet with local peoples for their problems and do constructive works prescribed to them. But it is the quality time rather than quantity time devoted to the family. Their work shows that incorporating a women's perspective in decision making should result in better decisions that reflect the needs and interest of the family. There are examples in the panchayat that many mukhias had made efforts to stop alcoholism, dowry, polygamy and atrocities on women and dalit peoples.

(b) Relief from Domestic Activities

It was also noted that among fifteen mukhia's in Kalyanpur block most of them belonged to joint family only 19.6 per cent were nuclear families. Most of them accepted that their household work was not affected by their new role because their paper works were done by their husbands and other family members. They only signed on papers. When they go in meetings they are followed by their male members from family. 40 per cent of them felt that it would be impossible for them to carry on their duty without the support of the family members. 20 per cent had accepted that their family and husband supported them in concluding family affairs and child rearing. Thus, small works like cleaning, sweeping dropping the children to schools, taking care of children and old members are done by husbands and family members.

The mukhia of Bahadurpur panchayat of Samastipur block gave all the credit to her mother-in-law who not only managed all household work but also took care of her children. So it was observed in the survey that women member backing from their family are doing their job satisfactorily but there are women representatives who have no support from family and husbands have to work hard for their political participation. They have to bear double responsibility and this affects their performance also.

(c) Challenges from Male Dominated Society

Women have to face the challenges of society also. Due to participation in outer work women had to bear the responsibility of the society also. They have to face criminals and bad elements of the society in performance of their duty. Most of the construction work; building work, planning work are captured by the criminals of the area. They want to influence the women members by their dreaded action. There are incidents of violence against women grassroots leaders in many places of working. They are generally attempted by men from privileged class or dominated class of the village. Because these people want benefits from women members, when women refuse to entertain them, they are made the victim of violences. These violences can be the result of caste rivalries. This is more common with women belonging to dalit class or backward caste. Women panches may also have to be the victim of abuses from the male panches. There are many reasons for this type of abuse reservation of sarpanch post for women, refusal of women members to the proposals of male members, their working system etc. are responsible for this type of crime. But in the Survey of most of the panchayats there was not a single incident of this type of abuse had been listened. There were no reported incidents of any physical assault on women panches or other members were reported. Though there were incidents of mental torture and abuses but not physical assault report was found. Some of the female members complained of men panches using double meaning languages in the office and meetings. Women also felt that they were new comers. In local politics with lack of political awareness, so they want to be guided by some one in politics. In Nagargama village Sarita Devi, Sarpanch had complained that when the male panches often fail in their politics, they began to harass the woman sarpanch. But the odd practice is ending because male members from their family are strongly beheld their women.

In the light of above statement it may be said that the Constitutional Amendment Act, 1992 has changed the social position of women also, especially in Bihar where 50 per cent reservation has made women self-confident and active in the field of political participation. Now, it can be judged that in day-to-day existence, women are not rendered powerless whether on the domestic front or outside in decision making processes. Woman can save her rights, her married life, her education, health etc. Now she can take part in any kind of action independently. She can also motivate the other women of their area about child rearing, nutrition, health, hygiene, sanitation and *swarojgar*. Their position in house and society is changed and become important. They can think the development of the villages. Many respondents are bold and active in solving the problems and they have also approached local leaders of political parties' MLAs and MPs for their problems. Bimla Devi, ward member of Kalonzar village became so bold that she could manage village politics in favour of women. She is now associated with many self help groups. So it may be said after observation that the district is improving in all aspects through PRIs.

Conclusion

In conclusion it can be asked whether women's entry into local politics through Panchayati Raj Institutions brought about qualitative changes in local administration?

It can be imagined on the ground of the fact that there are many qualities in women, different from men. It is said that women leaders would speed up the process of social welfare, honestly and seriously than men. They may also enhance public protection. It can also be analysed that due to their physical and mental structure they would act as a cohesive force to bring out social changes. Mahatma Gandhi wanted women to enter into politics as selfless, devoted social worker to undertake the crucial task of social reconstruction. By nature men are power grabber and women are selfless and can make sacrifices. So if these qualities came in politics and the politics will not be a game of corrupt power. From the sample respondents, the question of quality change through Panchayati Raj Institution representation was also asked in interview of local people, ward members, and panches. It was found that some women panches had been also involved in corrupt practices. So it was thought that in participation in Panchayati Raj Institution the quality of administration would improve, was not always true. There are many examples of the corrupt practices in Panchayati Raj Institution women members of all categories. One woman panch of Rahua Panchayat of Warisnagar block accepted that she did not avoid accepting bribe, because people were willing to offer it. Low education level and lack of proper information may also result in women unknowingly setting trapped into. But corruption and malpractice cases are very few in the district. It is also seen that most of the women representatives had protested against issues like corruption, bribe, dowry system etc. There are many examples that these women members were adamant and refused the illegal affairs. During the survey, a woman sarpanch of Ujiarpur block narrated how she was pressurised by the privileged person to issue him a licence to build a cow-shed in the village. In another case a woman mukhia had cancelled the licence of a dominant figure of the panchayat for illegal construction of road. So it may be said that women are always not grabbed and used as a tool. It is true that being a new entrant in politics, they become dependent on the male members who have been dominating the politics for years. But their political consciousness is increasing gradually and after 2006 Panchayati Raj election they come with a new get-up a confident nature and hard working social figure.

There are many areas where women panchayat members have made a better contribution especially in promoting primary education to girls, waste land development, road construction, sanitation and health, drinking water facilities, implementation of governmental schemes for children and women welfare etc. They have implemented certain schemes like RDA, DWACRA, DWCD, IRDP, TRYSEM, JRY, IAY etc. Besides many other schemes assisting women to improve the educational and nutritional standards of children. They are interested in improving old age pension scheme, widow pension scheme, cockpit and drain age, organising health camps, establishment of schools building in the village, establishment of self help groups and NGOs in the village etc. The survey showed that the women felt that they must do something for village. Many of them gave priority to solving the problem of water, irrigation, road light etc. in the village. But regarding gender cause, very few of them can answer in positive direction. Most of them had no idea of gender discrimination and no plan for upliftment of women. Because the male partners do not take interest in solving these problems.

There are problem as women members are not taken in important committees of the panchayats. Even matter related to women and children are not discussed with women members in panchayats. They also complained that lack of sufficient finance was a big problem for them in implementation of different development works.

So, it may be concluded that with the entrance in Panchayati Raj Institutions, women have been made self-realising and self-confident. The impact of the present Constitutional Amendment Act on women is seen in their development and progress both, physically and mentally. But they will have to go ahead for fundamental changes and development.

2

Panchayati Raj

Importance and Value in Democracy

In the words of Nehru, "If our independence is to reflect the people's voice, the greater the powers of the panchayats the better for the people." To provide power to the people and ensure people's participation in decision making process is the life blood of democracy. Panchayati Raj Institutions are prime means of decentralisation at grassroots level. There are three reasons behind it:

1. To prevent the pressure of relentless population.
2. The necessity of maximum utilisation of available resources for the development.
3. To promote people's active participation in the process of Democracy.

Democracy is much maligned and well accepted system of governance in which anyone from slum dweller to rich and elites are expected to be the equal participants in this system of the governance. It is called a government of the people, for the people and by the people. In the present age of globalization and liberalization the idea of 'for', 'of' and 'by' the people have been changed both, in its meaning, context and relevance. We often refer this as a transformation from centralized to decentralized system of governance in which the lowest ladder of public administration, i.e. Gram Sabha, Panchayat Samiti System have to play the dominant role in the management of the governance. Gram Sabha, the lowest body has the prime place in decision making, formulating and monitoring of developmental activities of the state through villages.

The greatest challenge before us is the election of good people as representatives. People with intellect and integrity, selfless and fearless and devoted to the welfare of the electorate. Unworthy people with criminal records self seekers have to be avoided. It is the fundamental principle of successful democracy. So it is our collective responsibility to find out such type of people from society, having idealism and courage of conviction among us and it can be possible through local bodies only.

Lecock said 'the distinction between local and central government lies partly in their relative constitutional positions and partly the nature of public services performed.' It is the fact that Constitution can only formulate laws for services but local organs by adopting these laws and regulations make a society stable and progressed. Local self government institutions especially PRIs in village administration may be called the cradle for democracy. They can provide the best training in good governance because local problems demand on the spot inquiry and quick solutions. This demand can be met, best by the local institutions, involving local people. They can try to bring awareness in the local people and can arouse their interest in problems of day-to-day activities of the locality.

These local institutions have very deep rooted in India. In old times every Indian village had a panchayat which used to function as an autonomous body. The panchayats were mostly free from the state interference. They were mainly concerned with administrative and judicial works and their working was so efficient and smooth that every village community was a sort of small republic. In this way true democracy was established.

The present structure of local government with PRIs was by the efforts of Lord Ripon, who has been called the 'Father of Local Self Government in India'. This system of local self government drifted without any change till the advent of Independence in 1947.

After Independence the local government may be said to enter into a new phase. The present Constitution came into force in 1950. The Constitution of India contains specific provisions of the progress of local bodies with special care of Panchayati Raj. The Directive Principles of State Policy also affirmed that state should take steps to organise village panchayats with full power and autonomy in village affairs. On 12th January 1958 the National Development Council endorsed the recommendation made by the Balwant Rai Mehta Committee on democratic decentralization for the genuine transfer of power recommended to three tier structure of local self government from the village to the district level.

States have evolved patterns of Panchyti Raj Institutions, suitable to their local condition and need in the light of the recommendations. Each state stands to benefit from the experiences of other and can add, alter or change its own system in order to improve its working. In pursuance of these directives nearly all the states passed resolution and today whole of the country has been covered with panchayats. Panchayat samitis are fully empowered to make budget and formulate schemes for village development.

Panchayati Raj aims to make democracy real by bringing the millions into functioning of democracy. It is a system of grassroots democracy which seeks to link the individual of remote villages to the central government. There are more than 579000 village panchayats in the country covering over ninety six per cent, inhabited villages and ninety-two per cent of the rural population of our country. There are about 4526 panchayat samitis of different nomenclatures at the block, taluka or tahsil level. There are about 330 zila parishads covering seventy-six per cent of the district in the country. Each zila parishad has an average thirteen to fourteen panchayat samitis and about 600 gram panchayats.

Name of the Body	*Number*	*Remark*
1. Village Panchayats	579000	92 per cent of the contries
2. Panchayat Samitis	4526	Block, Tahsil, taluka level
3. Zila Parishads	330	76 per cent of districts in the country

Source: Dept. of Rural Development *op cit*. Paras 4.4 and 4.5.

Till 1993 local government in India rested on the discretion of the states. The 73rd Constitutional Amendment Act has removed these lacunas. Article 243 of the Amendment Act defined zila parishad, gram sabha, panchayats etc. It refers to the power of Gram Sabha, constitution of panchayats, reservation policy, duration, working etc. The Constitution has now a new schedule—the XI Schedule, which is very important and deals with twenty-nine vital subjects for the working of PRIs. Part IX of the Constitution added in 1992, covers structural organisational, functional and financial aspects of the Panchayati Raj.

Panchayati Raj Institutions are the grassroots unit of self-government. They are the instruments for participatory democracy and decentralisation at the grassroots level. They carry back to the people the power that really belongs to them. Thus they have an immense potential for democratic decentralisation and developing power to the people. They are the vehicles of socio-economic transformation. This demands active involvement contribution and participation of people male and female in decision making process, implementation of developmental programmes and monitoring and evaluation of programmes especially for women, because they constitute fifty per cent of the rural population and this gives the right to them to participate and play an important role in the grass-roots politics of the villages.

In democracy decentralisation of economic, administrative and political power is essential because, a few centres of power cannot fulfil the needs of the vast multitude of people. For development and progress of the country people's active participation is a must. It means that people share the responsibility to accelerate the process of development. The process of development is itself multidimensional as well as multidirectional process. It encompasses area development, individual development as well as collective development. It is the reason that 'Father of the Nation', Mahatma Gandhi, had stressed that democracy must begin at the bottom. The local level problems cannot be solved in the meetings of officials and leaders in the five star hotels of metropolitans rather; it can be cured by the cooperation of local people with the help of these Panchayati Raj Institutions. We have examples of past when village panchayats played a pivotal role in the defence and development of villages in ancient India. They enjoyed vast power and made effective use of them with skill and innovation. They used to protect the people, collected the taxes for government, levied their own taxes to raise resources, services at times of calamities, organised educational institutions, looked after the people and supervised the manifold religious and cultural activities of the people. They had wide judicial power. Repetition of all these functions are the need of the hour and it can only be achieved through extension of the power and resources of PRIs, with men and women's equal participation.

After getting constitutional status in 1993, Panchayati Raj Institution brought about substantial changes in the existing acts and laws enacted by the respective state governments. Now regular and time bound elections of Panchayati Raj Institutions have been mandated and adequate devolution of economic and political power has been incorporated in the Act. Even central grants for development have been directly given to the Panchayats for avoiding delay and effective implementation of Schemes. Moreover provisions for reservation of S.C., S.T., backward castes and women have been made, which empower these people to take part in decision making and participating in the implementation of the schemes meant for panchayat. This is an attempt to attain the concept of Gram Sawraj visualised by Gandhiji. It is no doubt that in the present context only Panchayati Raj system can provide good governance.

Good governance is a dynamic concept. It encompasses fast changing political, social, economic and cultural atmosphere along with the international environment and conditions of operational governance. The basic constituents of good governance are accountability, administrative responsiveness, absence of discrimination on the basis of caste, sex, creed, culture, security, language, religion etc. PRIs are established to implement these factors in day-to-day life. In

Panchayati Raj Institutions—Gram Sabhas can accelerate the pace of development of infrastructure in the rural sector because it has been given immense power to execute the development work. Gram Sabha must take projects related to roads, energy, agriculture, housing, education, health, sanitation, fuel, fodder and women and youth training also. It can also make projects in the field of poverty alleviation and employment generation. For the structural transformation of a backward country like India and especially Bihar, it has been recognised that investment in education, health and infrastructure is essential for sustained growth.

Rural infrastructure development has been one of the most pressing needs of policy makers and administrators in Bihar. It is a multidimensional process which includes the development of socio-economic conditions of the people living in the rural areas and ensures their participation in the process of development for complete utilisation of physical resources for the weaker and poorer sections of society. It also enhances both, the capacity and capability of administration, socio-economic development agencies and agriculture, marketing units, working in the rural areas. Rural development is a strategy to improve this economic and social life of a specific group of people including small and marginal farmers, tenants and the landless. Panchayati Raj Institution may work as participating models of rural development for realizing the goals of democratic decentralization and people's participation. PRIs will be certainly helpful in this field also. A new opportunity has been provided by the 73rd and 74th Amendment Acts for decentralization of powers and empowering people leading to transformation of the character of our democracy from representative democracy to participatory democracy. The 73rd Amendment in particular has provided an opportunity to the people for participating in the process of governance and developments.

Participation of Women

Through 73rd and 74th Amendment Acts, women and weaker sections' participation in local body administration and in decision making bodies had enhanced. Before enactment of these Acts, women had occupied negligible percentage in Panchayati Raj Institutions. It was a landmark in the history of Panchayati Raj that women were provided with thirty-three per cent reservation in local bodies. In Bihar the Nitish Kumar government through Bihar Panchayati Raj Act, 2006 increased the reservation from thirty-three per cent to fifty per cent in the election of 2006 in Bihar. In this way about seven lakh women had been elected on different posts in all over Bihar. In the district like Samastipur a large number of women from different caste, class, group, religion and culture were benefited by the Act. They are large in number and they have to make decisions on the important issues of village upliftment including women and children. So it can be said that now PRIs has been the main source of empowerment to village women. Women had been granted fifty per cent reservation in each category. The schedule of reservation under different categories is as follows:

A. Women—50%

B. Extremely Backward Castes—20%

C. Scheduled Castes—16%

D. Scheduled Tribes—10%

(*Courtesy*—Hilor Maithili Journal, August 2006, pp. 15-16.)

The following table can present a wide picture of women's participation in the three tier Panchayati Raj System in Bihar.

Table 2.1

Sl. No.	*Members*	*Total Post*	*Women*
1.	Zila Parishad	1095	517
2.	Gram Panchayat	114852	15746
3.	Panchayat Samiti	11499	5344
4.	Mukhia	8405	3755
5.	Sarpanch	8405	3755
6.	Ward Members	—	—
	Total	144256	65117

Different Sections of Women's Representation

Total Number	65,117
Zila Parishad	19,95
Total women	517
Extremely Backward Castes	94
S.C. women	82
S.T. women	x
General women	341
Total	1,995
Panchayat Samiti	
Total posts	1,149
Total women	5,344
Extremely Backward	916
Scheduled Castes	804
Scheduled Tribes	40
General women	3,584
Panchayat Members	
Total posts	1,14,852
Total women	51,756
Extremely Backward castes	7,973
S.C. Women	7,372
S.T. Women	305
General Women	36,096
Mukhia/Sarpanch	
Total	8,405
Total Women	3,755

In this way it may be said that through reservation about sixty per cent women had now participating in the decision making process of the government. The poor, backward and downtrodden had got empowerment through this process of reservation. These resulted adequately in the direction of providing social justice to the poor people of the villages

So the basic aim of the Panchayati Raj Institutions are to execute development programmes with the help of local people, advancement of poverty alleviation programmes, nutrition programmes, public distribution system and ecological management are also entrusted to these panchayat bodies. Article 40 included in Part IV of the Constitution of India related to Directive Principles of state policy, requires the state to take steps to organize village panchayats and endow them with such power and authority. States are planned to adopt these measures for the development of the villages.

The powers given to PRIs as 29 subjects in eleventh schedule are very important and subjective. The separate part in IX schedule was added to the Constitution apart from article 243A to 243D. A fresh schedule XI enumerates the powers and the functions of PRIs. The adequate power and functions concerning the development of panchayat had delivered to the PRIs are very crucial and important. They are:-

1. Supervision of Primary Schools within the Panchayat's jurisdiction.
2. Supervision of Primary health centres within the area.
3. Appointment of Siksha Mitra in primary schools.
4. Appointment of Lok Sikshaks and Lok didis for the literacy and education to the children of scheduled caste and others within the jurisdiction of panchayats.
5. Implementation of Indra Awas Yojana and Jawahar Rojgar Yojana. The funds for these different yojanas are directly delivered to the panchayats.
6. Different development works, plans are initiated prepared and implemented by the panchayats, e.g. Kharnja Roads, water drainage system, village old wells reconstruction, roads repairing, sanitation etc.
7. Different works of integrated rural development programme IRDPs are executed by the panchayats.
8. The panchayats create, manage and coordinate different committees for the upliftment and welfare of the people. They are:

    (a) Administrative Committee,
    (b) Education Committee,
    (c) Construction Committee,
    (d) Health and Family Welfare Committee,
    (e) Planning and Development Committee.

9. Agriculture including agricultural extension.
10. Animal husbandry, dairy and poultry.
11. Fisheries.

12. Small scale industries including food processing industries.
13. Rural electrification and non-conventional energy sources.
14. Welfare of the weaker section and in particular of the scheduled castes and scheduled tribes.
15. Women and child welfare, family welfare.
16. Social welfare including welfare of the handicapped and mentally retarded.
17. Public distribution system.
18. Maintenance of committee assets.
19. Market and fairs.
20. Libraries.

Except above mentioned functions many other functions are performed by PRIs for the progress and development of the villages.

But it is not an easy task as they have been driven away successfully since our Constitution came into force. The bureaucracy has occupied the space vacated by people but it does not perform the role assigned to it as it has been oriented to act in accordance with the directions of the higher ups. Further populism has become the main stay in politics for securing votes and development has taken a back seat. But the 73rd Amendment Act brings a totally new paradigm which emphasised the fact that the beneficiaries have to be transformed with developmental participants. It has made participation a reality by creating a Gram Sabha in every Gram Panchayat which is an assembly of the people, who have registered as voters in the panchayat are by transforming the character of democracy. In this process a new rural leadership would emerge from among the people especially from the marginalized, the socially excluded categories like dalits and women committed to the upliftment of the poor, neglected, oppressed and unattended.

In this way it may be concluded that PRIs come forward to uplift the position of villages with adequate power. There are some hurdles and problems in the exercise of their power. These hurdles and problems are as follows:

The election of PRIs, was not held on party line in Bihar as in Tamil Nadu. So the desired and expected growth of PRIs has been marred and hampered due to the ruthless competition by state level politicians. Because the state level politicians used to see the representatives of PRIs as rivals in the constituency. They consider them as a threat to their hegemony in the area. It is a great hurdle in the way of proper functioning of PRIs.

Then the bureaucratic apathy is one of the serious bottleneck in the smooth functioning of the PRIs. Mostly PRIs representatives are uneducated and rustic and not well qualified so bureaucracy want to control and supersede these representatives especially in the case of women they always try to mislead them about different plannings and allocation of funds.

Another impediment to the PRIs success is the recent spurt in criminalisation of politics. Politics becomes a game of criminals. The Vohra Committee Report speaks volume about it, charging forty two MPs with criminal antecedents. In Bihar during PRIs election of 2001 many cases of murder and death were occurred due to criminal base of the candidate and politicians. Then Bihar government issued definite instructions to file FIR against the respective candidates in case of violence and murder, the result was very positive. There was zero crime in next phase of elections in Bihar. So, the entry of muscle men and person having criminal records has its toll on the smooth working of PRIs.

The corruption has its own toll on PRIs. Many mukhias and zila parishads are not hesitating in taking bribe in different plannings of government. They are doing illegal work even if people disapproved them.

There is no transparency and accountability in their functioning is being seen in their working.

Casteism is one of the malaise eating into the organs of PRIs. The dominated caste always wants to capture the weaker and dalit classes. Candidates are chosen not on their political efficiency or social work but by caste leaders.

Lack of sufficient fund is another hurdle in the field of the successful working of PRIs. It is satisfactory that funds are being given directly to PRI members. But they are not adequate in comparison to work loads. There is also a need to check the process of expenditure for transparency and accountability in the funds.

Gram Sabha, which is the primary organ of PRIs, should work efficiently and actively. Absentees and proxy presence should be stopped. Women representatives are not so serious in their responsibility, they are likely to be represented by their husbands or other family members.

Lack of the tools of E-governance is another problem. In this age of fast communication, when India is emerging as Information Technology super power. Most of the panchayats are lacking the facility of telephone, mobile, internet etc. and any kind of new information about projects and schemes are not reaching timely due to lack of information technology.

So, there are hurdles which most of the PRIs are suffering today. These hurdles interrupt the working of these institutions and the aim and objective for which these institutions are established is not fulfilled. But these hurdles and problems can be cured by proper guidance and training, proper education and personality building. Orientation and refresher courses should be arranged for members time to time. No doubt PRIs are the best pillars on which our democracy can stand successfully.

3

Bihar Political Atmosphere and Women's Role

A. BIHAR: POLITICAL ATMOSPHERE AND WOMEN

Bihar, a most populated state of India, is known everywhere for its backwardness. It is due to lack of proper guidance to the resources of the state. Bihar is not only backward in its utilisation of resources but politically also. Being the second populous state before the division of Jharkhand, it had fifty-four seats of MPs in Lok Sabha and 312 seats in Vidhan Sabha. But women's share is very low. For the 54 Lok Sabha Seats only 13 women contested from different constituencies in 1999 Parliamenty election. The ruling RJD had given only three seats to women. Parties like Congress and BJP which have claimed women's empowerment gave tickets to two women each only. The following is the figure of the representation of women in parliament in different elections.

Representation of women in Bihar Assembly from 1952 to 2001 election is 4.3 per cent. It is the fact that in Bihar women politicians also failed to establish a sustained and strong ideality in the national politics. They also did not motivate the other women to play an active participation in politics. There are many factors responsible for the low participation of women in politics, but the most important are the corruption and backwardness of the state in all fields like education, social, economic, cultural, political. Male dominated society is also not in favour of their active participation. Media has also not highlighted the contribution or achievements of women largely. If Rabri Devi became the Chief Minister of Bihar, it was not her contribution or merit but because of the position of being the wife of R.J.D. supremo Mr. Laloo Prasad Yadav. Like Rabri Devi, Anpurna Devi, Aruna Devi, Kanti Singh, Renu Devi etc. are the instrument in politics and their role is not very useful in society for women folk. But in past women like Krishna Sahi, Ram Dulari Sinha, Manorama Devi, Tarkeswari Sinha, Rita Verma had displayed individual political acumen.

Table 3.1

Year	Lok Sabha			Rajya Sabha		
	Total Seats	*No. of Females*	*Per-centage*	*Total Seats*	*No. of Females*	*Per-centage*
1952	449	22	4.9	219	16	7.3
1957	500	27	5.4	237	18	3.6
1962	503	34	6.8	238	18	7.5
1967	523	31	5.9	240	20	8.3
1971	521	22	4.2	243	17	7.0
1977	544	19	3.5	244	25	10.2
1980	544	28	5.1	244	24	9.8
1984	544	44	8.1	244	28	11.4
1989	517	27	5.22	245	24	9.7
1991	544	39	7.7	245	38	15.5
1996	543	40	7.36	223	20	9.0
1999	543	43	7.9	237	22	9.2

Source: Census of India 2001.

But now scenario is changed. During our pre-panchayat election tour in different blocks, we found the women of the region are making their share in politics. They were found gossiping with one another regarding the candidates of the election. This is a new trend. Because, before it these women were not interested in any political activity and political system, only their interest was found there, where women candidates participated, but they did not vote independently. Only a few high caste women were interested to talk about election prospects. Most of the dalit and weaker section women complained that their votes are used by the rich and dominant classes of the society. Due to *parda* system and other social problems high classes of women were also reluctant to go to the polling booths.

Though in the history of National movement, we can found that women of Bihar under the guidance of honourable Mahatma Gandhi participated whole heartedly in spite of *parda* system. But after independence, they are ignored and their contribution is forgotten in politics. While there have been a substantial number of new entrants among women candidates, a large number of the older ones have also dropped out from active participation in politics, while they come from families with long political traditions. These types of dropout indicated degree of disillusionment with the political process.

In the same way Muslims and tribal women show a lower level of participation, both as voters and as candidates, although there are exceptions to their rules also. Rather, women of scheduled castes have higher participation rate. In our observation we found them politically more conscious than other classes of the society, though they are not literally sound and culturally developed.

These low participation and low awareness in women in Bihar had factors, like:-

Caste Factor

Caste has played a significant role in the politics of Bihar ever since its creation in 1912. The land of Bihar comprises a number of castes and communities and every caste has its significant status in society. Rajni Kothari in her famous book *'Caste and Politics'* accepted that caste is the first determining factor of political process, but in Bihar it can be said that it is the foremost determining factor. It affected politics not after independence but before independence also. The British rulers had based their whole political process on the walls of caste. All the castes may be divided into three main groups.

The group of higher caste comprises Brahmins, Bhumihar, Rajput and Kayastha mainly because of their highest status in caste hierarchy and superiority in the field of education, learning, agriculture and politics. They dominate the politics of the area. The population of Yadvas in this state is about 11.5 per cent and they have ruled the state for fourteen years in the leadership of Sri Laloo Prasad Yadav, as dominant not only in politics but in all spheres of life. They are the most dominant and politically conscious among all the castes belonging to the middle group. In the same way in the lower group Dusadh is dominating caste especially in the leadership of Sri Ram Vilas Paswan and his family. So it may be concluded that women who have caste support can be politically conscious in Bihar. Ram Dulari Sinha, Rabri Devi, Ram Siv Kumari Devi etc. are the best examples of their sound and rich caste ground.

Table 3.2: Castes

Upper Castes		*Middle Castes*		*Lower Castes*	
Brahmin	Bhumihar	Yadav	Kewat	Dusadh	Chamar
Rajput	Kayastha	Mallah	Teli	Mushar	Dom
		Bania	Koiri		
		Kurmi	Mali		

Social, Cultural and Economic Position of Women

Any assignment of the status of women has to start from the social framework, social structure, cultural norms and value system. The most, important of these institutions are the system of decent family, marriage and religious traditions. They provide the ideology and theories for men's and women's notions about their rights and duties. And it is also a fact that social status of women in Bihar is a typical example of the gap between the actual position and roles accorded to them by the Constitution and the laws and these imposed on them by social traditions and culture. A woman is primarly associated with home affairs and whether they are working or non-working does not matter. Their role in the outside world has not yet been accepted till now. So decision making and the exercise of political power is still regarded as an exclusive male preserve. It is popular in middle classes of the society, politics is supposed to be the duty of men so women are kept aloof from it. After winning the election the women representatives have not shown serious concern in problems that affect women especially. This is because of the male dominance in the society.

The male members of the family try to solve the problems related to welfare issues in panchayats. The studies in different districts reflect that women were used as proxies. Because, they serve the patriarchal interests of the family. Most of them come in politics for protecting the constituency of their male relatives. So it may be said that due to male dominance in society, illiteracy, customs and traditions, the socio-cultural atmosphere are not in favour of women's participation in politics in Bihar.

Criminalisation of Politics

Bihar is a den of criminals of all castes and groups. Most of these criminals are attached with certain political leaders or party. An important factor why women dread to come to politics is because of the atmosphere of terror and horror of criminals especially in the rural areas. The deteriorating law and order situation and rising incidents of crime in politics compel woman from taking active part in political process. Man, money and muscle power play vital role in election and not every woman can be Phoolan Devi, Rama Devi. In such a violent and volatile political atmosphere women did not want to take part in politics.

Illiteracy

Illiteracy is a curse for women in Bihar. Due to gender inequality women's literacy rate is much below in Bihar, the figures of Table 3.3 explain the original outlook of the literacy rate of female in important stages in Bihar.

This is because the parents are more interested in the marriage of their daughters than their proper education. Most of the girls give up their study and make themselves active in household activities. Because of the custom of dowry and *Tilak*, it is felt that after promoting higher education to the girls, it will be difficult for parents to arrange their marriage. One of the major problems of rural educational system is the massive wastage and stagnation, generally termed as dropout. Female childrens, who are from socially and economically disadvantaged group, are prone to be dropout. In our observation it was found that in the total number of dropouts majority were females. There are government schools in villages but nearly 22 per cent of girls could not continue their study after primary school, 23.5 per cent of them continued their study up to the high school level and 8.5 per cent of the total female could reach the college level education in Bihar.

Table 3.3: Literacy Rate of Male and Female in Bihar

Year	*Male*	*Female*
1901	7.5	0.06
1911	8.56	2.5
1921	10.2	1.81
1931	12.5	2.01
1941	21.6	5.2
1951	21.8	4.4
1961	26.4	4.6
1971	32.5	4.8
1981	42.5	11.6
1991	46.5	17.8
2001	75.8	25.1

Source: Census of India 2001.

Table 3.4: Percentage of Female Dropouts

Education	*Percentage of Female*	*Dropout*
Primary level	22.0%	77.9%
High school level	25.5%	74.5%
College level	8.5%	91.5%

Among the caste groups of Hindus dropout was very heavy in the case of scheduled castes. It appears from the table that maximum percentage of upper caste females dropped their education after middle school level and only 7 per cent were admitted to colleges. In Muslims upper castes 25 per cent respondents attend their primary education, 37.5 per cent continued their education up to middle school level and 1.5 per cent join colleges. The main reasons for this dropout are gender inequality in the state. Non-availability of separate schools for girls, general feeling among the people of this area is that Government schools are not providing quality education, non-availability of high schools in every village because due to *parda* system parents do not want to send their daughters in other villages, early marriage of girls, expensive education etc. are the main factors for girl's dropout in villages.

The Bihar education project was launched in 1991. The basic aim of the project is to provide quality primary education for the children of age group of 6-14 years. But the process is going very slowly and illiteracy is affecting the socio-political aspects of women in Bihar.

Economic Dependence

Though women play crucial role in sharing and shaping of the economic structure of society in Bihar but their role is denied everywhere in the state. Agriculture is the main occupation in the state, about 70 per cent of Bihar's population depend upon agriculture. The rural women often called as farm women, constitute almost 50 per cent of farm workforce and play a significant role in Bihar agricultural set-up but denied their equal share. This is because of the discrimination of society and family. The discrimination is due to gender biasedness in the society, culture, traditions and social belief influenced the occupational discrimination among female workers. The employers in most cases prefer male labours rather than female. So the families of rural areas are economically not very sound in spite of their hard labour. They cannot bear the expenses of election or meetings. It is analysed that most of the women in politics come from well to do families. Working women including professionals have great awareness but this is not always reflected in participation. Low economic status mars the prospects of the political development in the society.

Role of Political Parties

In Bihar these are the factors responsible for low participation of women in political activities. Many national and regional parties are active, but they do not give proper and equal chance to women in election. The fact is that the political parties always play card on women's problem but neglected their task of politically educating and mobilizing women adequately. Therefore, it is a drastic increase in the number of independent women candidates. It is due to the failure of the parties to sponsor the women in elections. The parties generally want to seek the support of the male members of the family expecting that they will manage their women in election particularly in rural areas. In large cities same approaches have been made to oblige women voters but in rural environment it is not felt essential.

So it may be concluded that Bihar's political atmosphere was not very favourable for women candidates due to many socio-cultural and demographic features. Role of criminals in political atmosphere had made the half population to make a distance from the active politics. The duel personality of political leaders had also affected the political participation of women in Bihar. After observation it was found that they felt insecured in the present political atmosphere and therefore want to engage them in their day-to-day activities. There is some evidence of disillusionment among women with the political process because of this prevalence of corruption and inefficiency in political circles and because, women felt that politics could not solve the problems which affected their day-to-day activity. In a survey about 42 per cent women supported revolution for social changes and progress and 35 per cent opposed to the system of election. The majority felt that the biggest problems before the country are unemployment, poverty, illiteracy, rising prices, terrorism, corruption and breakdown of law and order etc. We should care for these problems rather engage in politics. They have shown their support against the rising prices, adulteration of food, unemployment, and social evils like dowry, foeticide, polygamy, atrocities on women etc. rather participation in politics. This is the reason that in Lok Sabha and Vidhan Sabha elections, the number of women participants is very low. In Vidhan Sabha also they is few in number. Table 3.5 shows the actual status of women in Vidhan Sabha from 1952 to 2005 election.

Table 3.5: Women's Representation in Vidhan Sabha 1952-2005 in Bihar

Year	*Number*
1952	3.6
1957	9.4
1960-65	7.9
1967-69	2.2
1970-75	3.8
1977-78	4.0
1979-83	3.7
1984-88	4.6
1989-92	2.8
1993-97	3.4
1998-01	4.3
2001-04	4.6
2005	4.8

If we want the equal participation of women as the half population of the state, the governmental and non-governmental efforts should be made. Reservation in different political posts should also be made. Tickets in election should be given to women equally with men and society should accept the position and role of women in politics.

B. THE LAND OF MITHILA : PHYSICAL STRUCTURE, POLITICAL ATMOSPHERE AND WOMEN

Mithila, one of the border areas of India, comprises over two hundred miles of India's frontier with Nepal and Bangladesh. So it may be said that Mithila is a region of high strategic importance in the Indian Union. It has got various names like—Tirbhukti, Videha, Tapobhumi, Sambhavi etc. In its historical background Mithila continued to be the centre of Aryan civilization for centuries. The standard of philosophical discussion in the court of Janak points to cultural tradition of Mithila. It has the unique privilege of being the birth place of Mahabir, fourth Thirthanker of Jainism. Geographically, it covers Darbhanga, Samastipur, Madhubani, Sitamarhi, Saharsa, Purnea, Kishanganj, Madhepura, Begusarai etc. The word 'Mithila' has been mentioned in various ancient literatures. It is believed that Nimi, the son of Manu, the king of Ayodhya, came to this land of sacrifices. His son Mithi founded a kingdom here, which he named Mithila. The land of Mithila is very fertile.

Since long Mithila has been a great centre of learning in the world. It has contributed remarkably to the study of Mimamsa of which there were two great scholars the Bhatta School and the Prabhakara school. Like Nalanda, Mithila attracted scholars from different parts of the country for advance and specialised studies in Nyaya and Logic.

The political atmosphere of Mithila is not different from other parts of Bihar, especially in Samastipur district. Like other districts, in Samastipur women are also in very few numbers interested in political participation. It can be proved that after independence to the present day, the number of women legislators or MPs is very limited. The Constitution of India made a deliberate radical departure from the inherited social system by giving women, equal social and political status but their position was not improved and they were kept away from the decision making processes, politically. Though Mithila has produced some illustrious and scholarly ladies like Bharti, Lakhima, Dhirmati, Vishvasadevi, Chandrakala etc. But the past history of women empowerment and awakenness is hidden in the present atmosphere. Now women are the second grade citizens in the area and they are kept away from any type of decision making and participation.

There are many factors responsible for it. Male dominated society, *parda* system, dowry system, polygamy, child marriage, poverty, illiteracy etc. are the main reasons behind this backwardness.

Credit goes to the Panchayati Raj Act, 2006, which reserved 50 per cent of the seats of all categories for women in the PRIs. The political empowerment of women resulting from the 73rd Constitutional Amendment Act had two features: firstly, there is a visible improvement in the administration and delivery of services at the Gram panchayat level.

Secondly, the Act had made contribution for women to gain social recognition and enable them to face age old repressive traditions and customs.

After a brief discussion with panchayat samiti members and mukhia, sarpanches' interview, it was found that they had become the role models for other women and girls. A women respondent Sangeeta Devi of the Kalyanpur block asked if Rabri Devi an uneducated woman can head the Bihar administration for 7 years, why we cannot manage the panchayats. She was very optimistic in her approach. One Sheela Devi of Dighara panchayat in Pusa block also accepted that after 2001 election of panchayati raj women of the panchayat became active, so it was found that in comparison to the Lok Sabha election of 1999 and Assembly election of 2000, women were more confident and enthusiastic.

In our observation, we found political awareness of women in the region increased. Following questionnaire and their answers can prove this changing attitude of women of this district.

Political Awareness of the Respondents in Assembly Election 2000.

Did you cast your vote in Assembly Election 2000?

Sex of Respondents	*Total No. of Respondent*	*Yes*	*No*
Female	150	47	103
Male	50	32	18
Total	200	79	121

Political Awareness of Respondent in Panchayati Election 2001.

Did you cast your vote in Panchayat Election 2001?

Sex of Respondent	Total No. of Respondents	Yes		No.	
		No.	Per cent	No.	Per cent
Female	150	112	74.7	38	25.3
Male	50	41	82	09	0.18
Total	200	153	76.5	47	23.5

These tables show the changing attitude of the women in this district. When asked whether they cast their vote in Assembly elections 2001, only 47 per cent women responded in 'yes', and when asked about panchayat election the response was 74.7 per cent. It shows the increasing trend in the political awareness of the women of the district.

In Mithila region caste plays vital role in political awareness. Maithil Brahmins are the dominating caste of this area. Yadav, Koiri and Dusadh are politically active in this region in Samastipur district. Out of 10 seats in Vidhan Sabha 6 seats are occupied by Koiri caste, who is dominating caste of the region.

It is a land of customs and beliefs. Cow, fish and water of Ganga have special significance in the cultural and religious life of the people in the region. It also affects their political life. So it may be concluded that Mithila is a region with glorious past in educational, political and cultural field but now moving for its identity.

4

Political Participation of Women in Samastipur District

Hurdles and Impediments

Political participation of women in India has been neglected even since independence. Though our country has adopted democratic system of government and the women constitute 48.9 per cent of population of the country, but their political participation is very low. Due to various constraints they could not occupy the positions of power and assume leadership roles. Women's representation in the Lok Sabha has never risen above 8 per cent. The cause of this low level representation does not lie in women's non-participation in politics. Table 4.1 explains the pattern of electoral participation of women in Lok Sabha in different elections.

Women's participation has been increasing rapidly but it is not satisfactory. They are also denying opportunities to participate in the administration, even in the making of decisions that affect their life and welfare. Though Father of the Nation Mahatma Gandhi had believed that women had a positive role to play in the reconstruction of society and the recognition of their equality was an essential step to bring about social justice. This added to the massive participation by the women in the freedom movement and had a direct impact on the political and social elite, including women. After independence, when the constitution was adopted women like Smt. Sarojini Naidu, Hansa Mehta, Renuka Roy, Durgabai Deshmukh etc. took part in the constitution-making. In our Constitution there is a guarantee of equality and dignity of the

Table 4.1: Pattern of Electoral Participation of Women in Lok Sabha

Year	Percentage of voting men	Percentage of voting women	Total Seats	Women seats	Percentage of women contested	Total seats	Percentage of women members
1952	53.00	37.10	51	23	45.09	499	4.40
1957	56.00	38.77	70	27	38.57	500	5.40
1962	62.10	46.63	68	35	51.47	503	6.70
1967	66.70	55.48	66	31	48.43	523	5.90
1971	69.70	49.15	86	22	27.50	521	4.20
1977	65.62	54.96	70	19	25.70	544	3.40
1980	57.69	51.22	142	28	19.70	544	5.14
1984	63.61	68.17	421	159	28.30	544	7.90
1989	70.79	43.90	189	28	14.80	525	5.30
1991	52.56	47.42	307	33	10.75	503	6.60

individual and it claimed the fundamental rights of women to political and legal equality and guaranteed non-discrimination in employment and office under the states. Our Constitution had provided many channels for the development and progress of the women. The preamble of the Constitution, the chapter of Fundamental Rights and Directive Principles of State Policies are among them. The safeguards from atrocities are the specific objectives for this purpose. These constitutional provisions are meant to empower the 48.9 per cent women population in India. But in practice, we find a wide gap between the stated social objectives and achievements, between the legal framework and empirical reality, between the symbolism and actuality. And this is the reason that after these constitutional safeguards and legal framework, the participation is still very low.

There are three indicators to assess the political participation of women:

1. Participation in the political process as the voters and candidates in election.
2. Political attitudes such as awareness commitment and involvement in politics and autonomy in political action and behaviour.
3. Their impact on the political process.

Participation in the Political Process

Participation in the political process can be judged by the position and number of voters and candidates in the election. Election statistics indicate a general trend of increase in the turnout of women voters. In country basis, their percentage increased from 46.6 per cent in 1962 to 55.4 per cent in 1967, 49.17 per cent in 1971 and 52.2 per cent in 1976 and 53.9 per cent in 1981, 54.6 per cent in 1987, 55.2 per cent in 1991, 56.3 per cent in 1997 and there was an increasing trend in other elections also.

In Samastipur district the number of women voters were also increased during different elections. In fourteenth general election of 2001, there was general decline in participation of all voters; but the number of women voters was increased. Though Samastipur district of Bihar is known for the educational and social backwardness of the women and their persistently low mobilization in election as voters, but their percentage was higher than male members of the society. Patterns of political behaviour from different blocks indicate influences of various interrelated factors, such as the social status of women, their economic position, their educational and cultural atmosphere and the overall regional outlook towards women's participation in the wider society. In the case of candidate, the difference between men and women is much sharper. No women candidate had ever contested for Lok Sabha in the district. The number of female MLAs are also very marginal, though there are ten seats of Vidhan Sabha falls in this district. It is not only in Samastipur district but Bihar as a whole had very low political participation in different Legislative Assembly elections.

Table 4.2 can prove the low participation of women in comparison to other states of the country. Even in Punjab where women voters have out stripped the men in the urban areas, had an extremely poor number of candidates. Though women in most of the states are very vocal in criticising the political parties for not sponsoring women candidates. Apart from election data, our discussion with different groups of women leads to certain general conclusions. The steady increase of women voters at each election shows that the response of women to the political rights conferred on them by the Constitution, in improving, keeping other things equal, development of literacy and mass communication may help to draw large number of women into the political main stream. Even in the 2004 Lok Sabha and 2005 Legislative Assembly elections number of Muslim women had also increased and took a keen interest in politics and participated regularly. Women of the intermediate and scheduled castes had higher participation in elections as voters. But there is a general feeling in the district that political parties had neglected their work of politically educating and mobilizing women perfectly.

Table 4.2: Women Representation in Bihar Legislatures 1952-1997
(% of Women MLAs)

State	*1952*	*1957*	*1960-65*	*1967-69*	*1970-75*	*1977-78*	*1979-83*	*1984-88*	*1989-92*	*1993-97*	*State Avg.*
Bihar	3.6	9.4	7.9	2.2	3.8	4.0	3.7	4.6	2.8	3.4	4.3
Andhra	2.9	3.7	3.3	3.8	9.1	3.4	4.1	3.4	3.7	2.7	4.0
Gujarat	-	-	8.4	4.8	3.2	Ne	2.7	8.8	2.2	1.1	4.2
Haryana	-	-	-	7.4	6.2	4.4	7.8	5.6	6.7	4.4	6.2
H.P.	0.0	-	-	0.0	5.9	1.5	4.4	4.4	5.9	4.4	3.6
J&K	-	Ne	0.0	0.0	5.3	1.3	0.0	1.3	Ne	2.3	1.5
Karnataka	2.0	8.7	8.7	3.2	5.1	4.0	0.9	3.6	4.5	3.1	4.5
Kerala	0.0	4.8	3.9	0.8	1.5	0.7	3.2	5.7	5.7	9.3	3.6
M.P.	2.1	10.8	4.9	3.4	5.4	3.1	5.6	9.7	3.4	3.8	5.1
Maharashtra	1.9	6.3	4.9	3.3	9.3	2.8	6.6	5.6	2.1	3.8	4.7
Punjab	2.2	5.8	5.2	1.0	5.8	2.6	5.1	3.4	5.1	6.0	4.0
Rajasthan	0.0	5.1	4.5	3.3	7.1	4.0	5.0	8.0	5.5	4.5	4.8
Uttar Pradesh	1.2	5.8	4.4	2.8	5.9	2.6	5.6	7.3	3.3	4.0	4.1
Delhi	4.2	-	Ne	Ne	7.1	7.1	7.1	Ne	Ne	4.3	5.9

Political Attitude

Levels of political awareness vary from region to region, from class to class and from community to community. They are maintained by the political culture of the area, the approach of political parties to women and the qualities of the local leadership. During the observation, it was found that the influence of education, urbanisation and exposure to mass media is not always uniform. Political awareness of women does not differ significantly between urban and rural areas. In Kalyanpur block of the district, education level is up and the block is supposed to be dominated by Koiri caste and Bhumihar caste. In most of the panchayats, women had greater awareness but this is not always reflected in participation. It is also found that there is not any positive relationship between higher socio-economic status and political awareness. In Rahua village of Warisnagar block, the political awareness is found less among women in the higher income groups. The influence of husbands and family members on women exercising their right to franchise seems to be greater, especially in villages like Somnaha, Jitwaria, Kalonzar, Bashudevpur, Gopalpur etc. of Kalyanpur block, the influence of village elders seem still strong. The scheduled caste women are mostly guided by their male associates in political matter and vote casting. The indifferent attitude of political parties is also responsible for the low participation of the women in election and other political activities. Though there are a number of women organisations and political parties, women cells, but unfortunately, they also failed to mobilize and provide political education to women. And this is the reason that women of this district are more concern with the problems of their day-to-day activities rather than political affairs.

Impact of Women on the Political Process

Women participation in politics has not been reflected in their record of success in election. The number and percentage of successful women candidates for the Lok Sabha has been declining steadily from 1962 to present election. It has generally been found that the success of women candidates depend upon party backing, campaign strategy adopted and personality including the family background of the candidates. After independence most of the women, who participated in the National Movement or in mobilizing the society became members of the central government or parliament. The women involved in state politics mostly come from the economic and political elite of state and their involvement in politics is due to political family and not for their social services. The absence of an active women's movement and failure of political organisation to mobilize women for the solution of their problems have always prevented women from exerting adequate pressure on political institutions. The small number of women in the legislature and their lack of position in the decision making bodies within the parties have limited their capacity to voice women's problem in these institutions. Most of the parties have tended to see women as followers of the males, rather their self-identity. And in the district, the leadership has become diffused and diverse, with sharp contradictions in their regard and concern for the inequalities that affect the status of women in every sphere, i.e. social, economic and political. While the position of some groups had changed for the better, the large masses of women continue to lack spokesmen in the representative bodies of the district. Though men recognised and advocate the desirability of giving equal opportunities to women in economic and political spheres, the norms and attitude regarding women's role in society remain traditional. While participation refers to direct involvement of people, both men and women in (i) decision making, (ii) implementation of developmental programmes, (iii) monitoring and evaluation of programmes, and (iv) sharing the benefits of development. These are the reasons that women want to discharge their traditional role and duty rather than participation in political processes.

So the political condition and participation of women in Samastipur district of Bihar was not satisfactory.

But credit goes to 73rd Constitutional Amendment Act 1992 as Panchayti Raj Act, which had given 33 per cent reservation to women in the grassroots democracy. 33 per cent reservation to women in PRIs had changed the socio-political scenario of the rural environment of the district particularly and the whole of Bihar generally. Now women of rural environment had got the political responsibility and realised the developmental goals for women's empowerment.

The equality guaranteed by the Constitution of India, demands active political participation by women which is integral to the whole issue of the progress of women. Women constitute half population in India which gives them the power to play an important role at the grassroots level. This participation is needed for following reasons:-

(i) To initiate, formulate and implement politics and programmes which will benefit women. It is found in observations that in most of the panchayats women were ignored and suppressed by their male counterpart.

(ii) To bring a feminine perspective to the process of planning, policy formulation and execution of rural development programmes, women participation is the need of the hour.

(iii) To empower the women folk of the village, empowering women refers to strengthening their innate capacities through acquiring knowledge, power and experience.

Women are the active agents of socio-economic transformation in rural areas. They can understand better their problems, identify them and are aware of strategies towards the solution. Larger participation will provide women an exposure to outside world. It will also provide a common platform for women to gain experiences to overcome their fear and enhance their decision making capacity. Hence their active participation will not only enhance the status of women in the villages but it will help in the development of the villages. At the Gram Sabha and Panchayat levels a new leadership would emerge which will do better administration and would provide constructive thinking in village administration and development.

The Balwant Rai Mehta Committee in its report supported the importance and value of women in the three tier structure of PRIs. It was suggested that women should find representation in the rural political institutions as co-opted members in panchayat samitis and panchayats. The three tiers of the Panchayti Raj System recommended by Mehta study team was:

> "Panchayat at the village level should be formed on an elective basis, with the reservation for scheduled castes, scheduled tribes and women."

While inaugurating the Panchayti Raj Institutions in Nagaur, Jawaharlal Nehru accepted that these institutions of Panchayati Raj are integral both to democratic self-government and to democratic development at the grassroots. He also emphasised that though Panchayati Raj Institution would make a revolution in village administration and process of decent realization it should work in natural cooperation. In political life everyone should be considered equal. There should be no distinction between men and women.

In the same way, the Ashok Mehta Committee in 1977 had also recognised the value of women in planning and implementation of rural development programmes. It also suggested a greater representation of women in panchayat bodies to influence progress and development. It recommended at least two women for Zila Parishad and Panchayat level either through election or co-opted members. In the light of the above suggestion certain reservations for women were made in states like Andhra Pradesh, Maharashtra and Karnataka. In the period of Mr. Rajiv Gandhi, a constitutional amendment bill called 64th Constitutional Amendment Bill was introduced and reservation of thirty per cent of the seats for women with tribal women, were also recommended. But due to vast controversy, the bill was defeated in Rajya Sabha. The historical step of reserving 33 per cent of seats in PRIs is a praiseworthy step of the government as the 73rd Constitutional Amendment Act, 1992. The Act came into force from April 24, 1993. It had added a new dimensions and directions to the process of democratic decentralisation and had also added new roles and responsibilities and power and functions to the Panchayati Raj Institution in India. It imposes constitutional compulsion on the states to develop political administrative, financial and developmental functions to grassroots levels to make democratic decentralisation a concrete reality. Being the half population of society, women are also involved in different processes.

The National Perspective Plan for Women (1988) also emphasized on the women proper participation in political process for their equity and social justice. It suggests 30 per cent reservation for women in Panchayti Raj Institutions. The champions of the Panchayti Raj desired that rural women should not only become the beneficiaries of development but more importantly the contributors to it. In its plan on the status of women the committee stressed that there should be reservation of 30 per cent seats for women in all rural local self-governing bodies at all levels from the Gram Panchayats to Zila Parishads. There should also be reservation of 30 per cent of the executive heads of all bodies from Gram Panchayats to Zila Parishads for women. There should be reserved constituency for all categories of women in all categories of seats of rural local self-government.

In the same way the committee on the status of women in India appointed in 1971 also recommended reservation for women to enhance their political capacity and decision making processes.

The present Constitutional Amendment Act, 1992 reserves 33 per cent seats in PRIs for women and after passing the Bihar Panchayati Raj Act, 2006 the present government of Bihar had reserved 50 per cent seats in all categories of post in local self-government of rural environment. It will provide an opportunity to ventilate their grievance and to take active part in the formal political arena which not only deals with social and economic problems but problems related to women and children also. The election to the PRIs has brought rural women to the main stream of society and they are trying their best to prove themselves efficient. They may have played a dummy role in the whole political processes of the village. It can be also said that large numbers of them are working under the pressure of their husbands and other relatives. In observation it was proved that about 90 per cent women of all categories in PRIs, educated or uneducated, rich or poor, upper caste or lower caste playing in the arms of their counterpart or relatives. This is not only in the district of Samastipur or in Bihar but perhaps most of the states of the country. State like Maharashtra and Karnataka are not abiding from this. On 17 August 1999, a woman sarpanch of Lakshmidupet, in Warangal district of Andhra Pradesh was beaten up by villagers because she had made a statement on village affairs against their wishes. There are many cases of atrocities on women representatives in PRIs by villagers and colleagues. But it is believed that this situation would not continue long. Women will be able to understand their political obligations and power by proper training awareness campaigns, political education etc. Though in most cases, they are housewives and first time entrants in politics, most of them are illiterate or educated upto primary level. They cannot take decision herself and 'Mukhiapati' and 'Sarpanchpati' are functioning in many panchayats. But the situation is changing. Especially, after 2006 Panchayati Raj election in Bihar women are proving themselves capable of participation and decision making policies. Mukhia of Jhawari Panchayat Chanchala Devi not only participates in meetings regularly but also takes decision of her own. There are many examples of women's active participation in the decision making process after enhancement of the Constitutional Amendment Act 1992 came into knowledge in the observation.

The statutorily reservation of seats for women in Panchayati Raj Institutions provided an opportunity for their formal involvement in the development and political processes at the grassroots level and influence the decision making process in the local governments.

Good governance is the need of democracy. These institutions could be able to change governance in India to good governance. Women can be elected to local institutions in large numbers as a result of this amendment. By 1994, 330,000 women had entered in politics through PRIs election. Through reservation in PRIs about 8 lakh women are elected on different posts of PRIs in the country. The percentage of women at various levels of political participation has sifted from 4-5 per cent to 40-45 per cent after this reservation. In Bihar after 50 per cent reservation it is about 56 per cent.

There are many examples, that now these women representatives had changed the governance by raising the issues of water, alcohol abuses, education, health and domestic violence. Though in different blocks of Samastipur district, this change is seen in few numbers, but these women representatives are trying their best in solving these problems.

The political participation of the women of this district can be judged by the following factors:-

Awareness Among Them

As the awareness is concern, there is a high degree of indifferent and vague conceptions exhibited by women in general, who simply cannot see to understand that how this Act can change their political attitude and rights and how constitutional provisions can make a difference in their political awareness. This feeling was found to increase with the geographical isolation of the village, poverty and illiteracy. In the Rahua village of Warisnagar panchayat where president and ward member both were women showed very little awareness about the panchayat. The male members of the family allowed their daughter-in-law to contest election because of reservation of seats for women but due to *Parda* system they did not allow their *'Bahu'* to go to Panchayat or outside the house. The lack of basic idea about the composition, functions and other activities of panchayat was common issue in women representatives. After observation, it was found that women only knew that panchayat should be there to solve their problems and provide different facilities to the villagers. After consulting the villagers most of them had complained that the president and ward members were providing facilities to their relatives and caste men instead of needy persons. They are working in the pressure of their caste men or the dominating personalities of the villages. A ward member of Kalyanpur block was caught in taking bribe for the contract of drainage in the village. The women members on the other hand complained that they were helpless and powerless as they had not got any power till now. People are less aware of the working of Gram Sabha in many Panchayats and the role of women members in these institutions, but in Kewta Panchayat of Dalsingsarai block, it was found a strong presence of women activists who are very active and sensitive to not only women problems but other socio-economic problems like dowry system, road, light, population control, education etc. Some representatives of different Panchayats asked for environmental and global problems also, which is a good sign of political awareness. So it is seen after observation that PRIs have created political awareness and financial indepedence among women. But besides these all benefits, women of these blocks showed very little interest in participation in political activities due to male dominance in the society.

Decision Making

Decision making capacity makes a man self-confident and powerful. Though the level of political awareness was found different in blocks they were influenced by the culture of the region but onething was similar among all the women that they cannot stand themselves in decision making process. This process was found missing among all spheres of women. Even in their decisions on home affairs they cannot take it alone. Some women, however, felt that they had more confidence in decision making on common issues like roads, temple, education etc. But in the field study, it was found that husbands, fathers and other relatives were considered primary decision makers. When asked the causes for not giving the right of decision making to women these persons had accepted that women are both vulnerable and aggressive. It needs protection and care, her aggression needs control. 80 to 90 per cent of decisions for the working of the panchayats are taken by the male members. Even among the very few, very vocal and vigour women leader keep their own decision and took the decision of contesting election. Vimla Devi M.Sc. and a political party activist was seen very bold about women participation and problems and contested on a general seat for Zila Parishad.

She has been involved in active politics since 1995 and her aim is to do something for the society especially for women. There are women who formed self help groups in the villages and take active part in local political activities, but they denied in sharing election because of their family traditions. It was seen that economic empowerment influences not only in the decision making processes but in the whole spheres of life. Lady Mukhia in Jhauri Panchayat of Kalyanpur block agreed that she has not much power or capacity to take any decision by herself. Though she is educated and understands the mode of administration, but her husband and other family members compelled her to obey them in decision making processes. Likewise her other activities in the Panchayat are also influenced by her husband. She also argues that women should come forward to take different activities of Panchayat. These women members are not called in general meetings and kept away from it because either they were not informed about the meetings or they were busy in their day-to-day activities.

After enactment of the 73rd Amendment Act, the women are conscious for their political rights and obligations. One Munia Devi of Morsand village of Samastipur block posed some very important loopholes which need to be redressed, if PRIs are to be effective for women. Many members had suggested measures for their better participation. According to them information network has to be strengthened. Women should be informed about reserve seats much before elections are due. This will go a long way in preparing women for the posts. They also demanded that every information regarding panchayats should be given to them. Some participants stressed for transparency in fund utilisation and allocation in the panchayats. So after the enhancement of the Act a large awareness in the political participation was found in different panchayat women.

Aspirations

Elected women in most of the villages are awakened. They began to take the things in their knowledge. They have great aspiration from the society and PRIs. Women who win for second time, are found full of confidence and asking for more information from panchayats. They demanded that more finance to panchayats should be granted because panchayats have to do a lot of developmental and progressive works for the villages. They are also asking for help from the society to lend consent and sustained support to the panchayat activities. They are very serious for developmental work which they got through XI Schedule to the Constitution. When some male members of Dighra village wanted to construct a temple on public land the Mukhia of that panchayat with her associates forced authorities to build a primary school on it. In another case also a woman ward member of Nagargama Panchayat of Dalsingsarai block raised her voice in favour of a road construction on a controversial land. There are examples that can prove the political participation of women in the district. Asked about reservation most of these women favoured it and wanted to continue it in other governmental organizations also. They also emphasised on workshops and training for their greater participation.

So in the matter of sensitisation, women openly expressed their positive thinking about the working and future of Panchayati Raj Institutions. They are fully understanding that due to Panchayati Raj Institution, they are politically empowered and socially valued. Mukhia, Sarpanch and even the ward member are called Netajee in their constituency and they feel themselves prestigious in the society. So PRIs had proved the best means of women empowerment.

Problems and Impediments

Though Panchayati Raj Institutions seem to be the best means of women empowerment and participation and through these institutions about 8 lakh women of the country are benefited and get empowerment, but there are problems and hurdles which women representatives have to face in discharging their day-to-day activities. These hurdles and problems are of double natured.

(a) Environmental Problems and Hurdles
(b) Individualistic Problems and Hurdles

(a) Environmental Problems and Hurdles

The social and political environment of the district is not in favour of women active participation in political activities. In the process of observation, it was found that, many women Mukhias and Sarpanches had agreed that they have not much knowledge and capacity to take decision by themselves. They accepted that before making any decision on any vital issue, they consult their husbands and other family members. There are many among them who accepted that issues related to their domestic affairs are also discussed by their husband and family members. They fight the election because their husband and other family members want to their participation. But this participation is not for women empowerment rather for safeguarding the seat, which is female seat in rotation process and next time it will be of general category then they (males) can contest freely and fairly. So like in other matters here also women are used as a tool of men.

The political capacity can be judged by planning process, its implementation and lastly, by delivering of the process. And in all stages we find lacking in the role of women. The studies of different Panchayats reflect that women are used as proxies. Because, their entry in political field is to save the seats and constituency for their male relatives and the decision to participate in election is not their own. This is the root cause that male members of the family always dominate the women members either Zila Parishad or panchayats. These women have no experience of active politics and male members of their family are involved in discharging the political responsibilities of political activities. Their proxies suffer from certain characteristics, such as:

(a) They display a lower level of political awareness.
(b) They feel their primary legality to their family.
(c) Their role as an elected representative is merely extension of their household role.

(d) They entered in politics to save their family member's seat in next election.

A study of the role of women in Panchayati Raj Institution in different panchayats of the sampling villages found that, majority of women panches were housewives and were either illiterate or very low educated. This gives opportunities to their family members to involve in village politics. After 2006 election of PRIs, in Samastipur district the institutions of 'Sarpanchpati' and 'Mukhiapati' were created which had no legal sanction but it was growing fastly in different panchayats. These 'Mukhiapati' and 'Sarpanchpati' used to coach their women members to speak at meetings and do their work properly when the women are illiterate. This is the reason that women panches of the panchayats were not interested to contest again as they felt that male members of their family did not allow them to function independently.

There is a big problem of the importance of caste in the elections. Rajini Kothari in her book *Caste in India* accepted that caste plays a vital role in the present setup of democracy in India. It also plays an important role at grassroots politics. Before reservation, the dominant castes of these villages captured the whole political system. The dominant caste leaders want to make pressure on their caste men to choose the candidate on their advice. Candidates are not chosen on performance, education and ability rather they are chosen by their loyalty to dominant caste leaders.

The elections of PRIs are not held on party line in Bihar as in Tamil Nadu. So the desired and expected growth of PRIs has been marred and hampered due to the ruthless competition by state level politicians. Because the state level politicians see the representatives of PRIs as rivals in the constituency. They consider them as a threat to their hegemony in the area. And women are the main sufferers of these trends.

Another impediment to the PRIs, women members' success is the recent spurt of crime in politics. Politics become a game of criminals. The Vohra Committee Report speaks Volume about criminalization of politics. Women members take fear of these crimes and wanted to keep themselves aloof from any kind of political activity. The entry of muscle men and criminal recorded persons into the election of panchayats mars the prospect of women candidature.

Then the bureaucratic apathy is one of the serious problems of women members in PRIs. Study in different panchayats shows that large number of PRI women representatives are not fully educated. They come from rural environment and are not aware of any kind of administration. They do not know the proper way of planning, budgeting and availability of funds. So they depend upon officials in performing their day-to-day working. These officials always try to misguide them. They want to control and supersede them. Especially in the case of dalit women, their attitude is not cooperative. In Jitwarpur panchayat of Samastipur block about 42 per cent PRI women members had accepted in interview that when they want to know the new plans and projects of development the officials do not cooperate them and always try to misguide them. The panchayat is Yadav and scheduled caste dominated and Mukhia and Sarpanch are also Yadav. But they do not want conflict with officials.

Lack of sufficient fund is another hurdle in the plan of successful working of PRIs in the district. This is not the problem of Bihar but of the whole country. In the Constitutional Amendment Act provision for separate finance committee for PRIs are made. But most of the states had not implemented it. The women members want to project development schemes for panchayat but due to lack of fund, schemes have not been completed in time. The Bihar Government had sanctioned funds directly to the Mukhia and Presidents of different institutions, it is a good sign of development but these funds are inadequate for works to be done. There is also a need to check the process of expenditure for transparency and accountability about the funds.

Lack of the tools of E-Governance is another problem. In this age of mass communication, when India is emerging as Information Technology supreme power, most of the panchayats are lacking the facilities of telephone, mobile, internet etc. Due to lacking of these facilities, any kind of information regarding planning, funding and implementation of schemes and projects are not reaching timely to the panchayats. There is great lack of power supply in this district as a whole. The position of villages is worst in this matter. They got 2 to 3 hour power in 24 hours. So any kind of information from telephone or mobile or internet is very difficult to them. The PRI members cannot communicate themselves on vital issues.

In the same way, the interference of local body administration is another disturbance, because they always try to establish their control over the decisions of the working of the panchayats. They make pressure on women members to arrange contract for their henchmen.

In spite of these environmental problems, there are individualistic problems also, which are of very serious nature and must be removed for successful working of PRIs.

(b) Individualistic Problems

In order to secure women's equality, status and dignity in all fields, there is an urgent and continuing need for changing societal attitude and elimination of all forms of gender based discrimination in the mind of men and women in the society. Their political participation could not be meaningfully understood by their physical presence alone. They have to face many obstacles like lack of family and social supports, the traditional and cultural barriers, the laws and customs of the male dominated society, illiteracy, poverty, lack of political awareness, lack of decision making capacity. Lack of managerial skills are imperative for the leaders to manage the personnels and the resource within the established framework of administration.

The physical empowerment could not meaningfully be understood by member's physical presence alone. This physical presence had nothing to do with the political situation of the panchayats. Because, women are not free to judge the circumstances of the panchayats. They have to depend on family. It was observed in survey that 66 per cent women members are of the age group of 30-45. There is a predominance of younger women in grassroots politics. 'Prayas' an N.G.O. is active in the survey of younger women in politics also noticed that women in the child bearing age group are coming forward to join politics in spite of the domestic responsibilities.

The burden of women has increased, she has to carry her household work, look after her children and old relatives and also attend the meetings and panchayat works. They are working with their male pertners for the development of the panchayat but, panchayat do not pay any salary or allowance to them. So it is natural that they give more attention to their family work than panchayat work.

Lack of proper training and guidance is a big problem of women members. Today administrative work became very complex. Now politics is also not a simple game, it has become the den of criminals. A woman representative due to lack of proper training and understanding find herself unable to tackle these problems. Because with the increasing emphasis on rural participation panchayats are expected to play an important role in planning and development, social welfare, education and in cultural activities. The total representation in Panchayati Raj Institutions is about 56 per cent in the district.

Illiteracy is a matter of great concern for PRI members. 67 per cent of the members of different categories are either illiterate or middle passed, 77 per cent of these members had education up to primary level only. Lack of education of women is an important cause of the exploitation of women. And it is found common in lower class and scheduled castes mainly.

Male dominance in society is a great social factor that makes a women member unimportant in the eyes of society. Though reservation was made and through reservation 50 per cent women came into the main stream of political processes but it is not favoured by male dominated society.

The social attitude is not changed so far and women are supposing inferior in society.

Political participation of women is severely limited due to a nexus of traditional factors. There are the domination of Indian politics by considerations of caste, class, religion, feudal and family status etc. The low participation in election and political activities appears to be the prevailing socio-economic conditions and biological make up of women on the one hand and traditional and conservative outlook and general backwardness among the masses on the other.

It is also well known that the present day election scenario has come to be a game of money and muscle power. This is a very alarming situation, which resisted women to come forward, particularly those who came from poor and dalit class, who had no previous political background. So they want to keep themselves away from politics. Those women, who can manage money and muscle power can contest in election. Though reservation has given them the right to contest but the social and political situation of the area is not very favourable for them.

The indifferent attitude of political parties is also responsible for low participation of women in political process of the district. Women involvement in decision making bodies of various national parties is not very encouraging, in fact, a majority of women, who are actively engaged in politics, have had either husband or other close relative in politics. The under-representation of women can be attributed to the great amount of conservation shown by all political parties. Because women are not considered to be winning candidates.

The top decision making position remain largely with male dominated and women had little influence. The lack of women's participation in political decision making has important consequences. It deprives women of important rights and responsibility as citizens and makes them aloof from their perspective and interests from policy making and decision making. Their voice is ignored. Credit goes to Seventy-third Constitutional Amendment Act which enhances the position of women by giving 33 per cent reservation to them.

So the women representatives have to face a lot of problems in their functioning of day-to-day activities. Women leaders hailing from literate upper middle class families can tackle the problems of administration to some extent because their social status and education help them. But women coming from poor and dalit classes, mostly uneducated and illiterate are economically and socially not in a position to understand the norms of administration. They have to depend on their associates for functioning. There is a great problem of communication, women representatives have to face. Lack of managerial skill is an imperative for the leaders.

Panchayti Raj Institutions come forward to empower women of the society. There are problems and hurdles, no doubt. They need to be visualized in a proper perspective. Most of these problems and hurdles can be removed by the proper guidance and training to them.

To overcome the problems the women's leader capacity has to be enhanced. A feeling which has been created over centuries to work against the interest of women cannot be changed immediately. The women have to build themselves in a position to prove themselves efficient and effective. The socio-economic and cultural environment must be changed in favour of women.

Government has to take serious steps for women's education and training. It is a matter of satisfaction that government has been making efforts to enhance the personality of women with the financial support of UNICEF and its own resource orientation courses and refresher courses should be organised time to time to make them able in decision making. In Tamil Nadu through the assistance of NGOs, government had changed the political scenario. About 40 per cent women members have started moving out from the clutches of their male partners. In Bihar the situation was changed in 2006 PRIs election in which 50 per cent seats were reserved for all categories of women. It should be maintained in other states also. The orientation and training programme should be given to Universities for proper implementation. The Universities will arrange the orientation, sensitization, capacity building, information and counselling programmes for women representatives for their proper and smooth functioning. Through the proper presentation, they can establish themselves in society and will find out proper remedies. There is every need and necessity to encourage them to improve their efficiency so that the institutions can be managed properly.

5

Role and Impact of Panchayati Raj Act 1992 on Women Political Empowerment

The Panchayati Raj Act passed by parliament in December 1992 is a major milestone in the history of rural local self-government. It is an act of political and administrative centralisation and releases the local population from control of bureaucrats and politicians. This act has not only enhanced the importance and power of PRIs but also given them constitutional status. Article 46 of the Constitution, which deals with Directive Principles of State Policies had endowed the panchayats with such power and authority as may be necessary to enable them to function as units of local self-government.

The history of local self-government in India is not new. These institutions are originated when the country was under British rule. But it did not enjoy any self-government either at the centre or state level. But today under the banner of self government, the country enjoys self-government both at centre and state level. In ancient times also the panchayats had to play vital role in village administration. They exercised power in various spheres such as administrative, commercial, industrial, and social including civil education and religious functions. In the present structure and style, it is the contribution of British Government. Local self-government in India, in the sense of electorals, enjoying wide powers of administration and taxation. The ancient village communities were constituted on a narrow basis of hereditary privilege of caste closely restricted in the scope of their duties, collection of revenue and protection of life and property were their main functions. They were neither the part of political education nor important part of the administrative system. A beginning of local government had started in 1687, when for the first time a local governing body Municipal Corporation was established in Madras. But it was flourished in the time of Lord Rippon. Another significant stage in the history of local government was the publication of the report of Royal Commission in 1909. In 1918, the Government of India issued the resolution in which it was accepted that the objective of self-government is to train the people in the management of their own local affairs and the political education of the people of locality. There are some areas of development which are strictly local in character and which require local knowledge, local initiative and local action. Therefore, participation of the local people in these institutions is a must. J. Laski rightly mentioned that "we cannot realise the full benefit of democratic government unless we begin by admission that all problems are not central problems and the result of the problems is not central in their incidence require decision at a place and by the persons, where by whom incidence is most deeply felt." It emphasised on that panchayats should be revived in the villages. Local government should be made broad-based by suitable extending the franchise. The president of local body should be elected not nominated. The Government of India Act, 1919 inaugurated an era of new interest and activity in the field of local government. The local bodies made free from many restrictions in respect of preparation of budget and many other powers. Men like Jawaharlal Nehru, Sardar Vallabhbhai Patel and Purushottam Das Tandon entered into municipal councils. The local government was moving in the direction of democracy.

The independence of the country in 1947 had taken a new turn in the history of local government in India. With the termination of British rule there was self-government at all the levels central, provincial and local. A conference was held in which Jawaharlal Nehru expounded the vital role of local government in free India. He remarked, "Local self-government is and must be the basis of any true system of democracy. We have got rather into the habit of thinking of democracy at the top not so much below. Democracy at the top may not be a success unless you build on the foundation from below."

As the present Constitution came into force in 1950, the local government may be said to have entered in a new phase. The Constitution allotted local government to the state list, the directive principles of state policies also affirmed state shall take steps to organise village panchayats to endow them to function as units of self-government. So the main objective of the local government is the greatest good of the greatest number. The team for the study of community projects and National Extension Service popularly known as the Balvant Rai Mehta Committee had made a mile stone in the field of local government. This committee was set-up with a view to ensuring economy and efficiency and for the arrangement of the programmes of community development. The Committee in its report published in 1957 had accepted that the community development and national extension service programme had failed to evoke popular initiatives. The Committee also recommended decentralisation of responsibility and power to the levels below the state. It recommended a three tier system of rural local government, namely village panchayat at the village level, the panchayat samiti at the block level and the zila parishad at the district level.

After Balwant Rai Mehta Committee report legislation was enacted in different states to make provisions for establishment of local government in their area. Till 1985, 12 states and Union territory had adopted the system. The structure, electoral system, power and function were differing in every state. Today more than 2,17,300 village panchayats in the country covering over 96 per cent of about 5.79 lakh inhabited villages and 92 per cent of rural population of our country are established. There are about 4526 panchayat samities in block level and 330 zila parishads covering 7 per cent of the districts in the country, each zila parishad has on an average 13 to 14 panchayat samities and about 660 gram panchayats.

Table 5.1: Zila Parishad

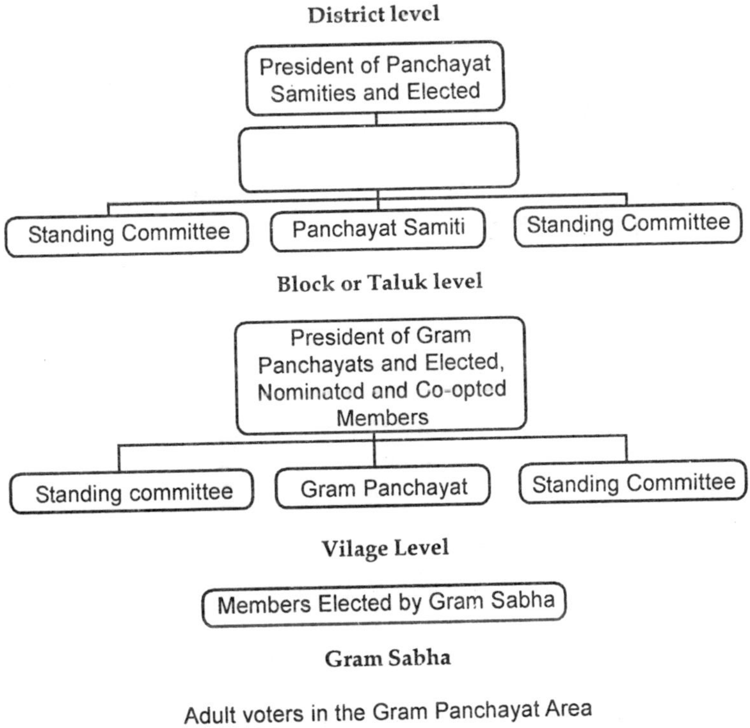

After Balwantrai Mehta Committee report legislation was enacted in different states to make provisions for establishment of local government in their area. Till 1985, 12 states and Union territories had adopted the system. The structure, electoral systems, power and function were differing in every state. Today more than 2,17,300 village panchayats in the country covering over 96 per cent villages and 92 per cent of rural population of our country are established there institutions. There are about 4526 panchayat samitis in block level and 330 zila parishads covering 7 per cent of the districts in the country, each zila parishad has on an average 13 to 14 panchayat samitis and about 660 gram panchayats.

The functions have been given to panchayats including village roads, community wells, maintenance of public parks, tanks, irrigation work, public hygiene, drainage and other civil services in some states. They had also been given responsibility for primary education and primary health care centres, women and child welfare and many developmental projects of village people. But till now the recommendation of these institutions have not got constitutional status.

Name of the body	Number	Remarks
1. Village panchayats	579,000	92 per cent of the country is rural population
2. Panchayat samities	4526	Operating at the block level
3. Zila parishads	330	76 per cent of the districts.

Since April 1993, local government in India both, rural and urban, has got constitutional status. In 1992 the parliament passed the Seventy-third and Seventy-fourth Constitutional Amendment Bills which came into force on 24 April 1993 in India.

Through 73rd Constitutional Act a three tier structure of rural local government was provided at the village, intermediate and district levels throughout the country. The concept of Gram Sabha has been incorporated in the Act. Gram Sabha is the assembly of village people, who are voters in the panchayats. It is the bottom of the village politics. According to Article 243(a) of the Constitution it is through Gram Sabha that representation is made accountable to the villagers. The chairman of a panchayat, the intermediate level and the zila level should be elected by and from among the elected members of this institution. Gram Sabha is the heart of the whole system. The legislation provided for a uniform three tier Panchayati Raj System at the villages intermediate and district levels.

While the chairman of a panchayat at the intermediate and district levels should be elected by and from among the elected members; the mode for election of chairman of panchayats at the village level shall be decided by the legislature of the state.

The most important and praiseworthy point of this Act is that the legislation provided for reservation for scheduled castes and scheduled tribes should be in proportion to their percentage in the total population of the area. And among this, one-third seats should be reserved for women members. These reservations will be on rotation basis. In the same way one-third seats of the office of the chairman will be reserved for women, and it will be also on rotation basis.

Reservation of seats for disadvantaged group of society especially for women and dalits will empower these sections. Because there are twenty-nine vital subjects for empowering these disadvantaged groups. The powers that had been given to Panchayati Raj Institutions are very wide and important. These powers cover all the developmental aspects of life. Some of these powers are:

1. Agriculture including agricultural extension.
2. Land improvement, implementation of land reform, land consolidation and soil conservation.
3. Minor irrigation, water management and water shed development.
4. Animal husbandry, dairy and poultry.
5. Fisheries.
6. Social forestry and farm forestry.
7. Minor forest produce.
8. Small scale industries.
9. Khadi village and cottage industry.
10. Rural housing.
11. Drinking water.
12. Fuel and fodder.
13. Roads, culverts, bridges, ferries, water ways and other means of communication.
14. Rural electrification, distribution of electricity.
15. Non-conventional energy sources
16. Poverty alleviation programmes.
17. Education including primary and secondary.
18. Technical training and vocational education.
19. Adult and non-formal education.
20. Libraries.
21. Cultural activities.
22. Markets and fairs.
23. Sanitation including hospitals, primary health centres etc.
24. Family welfare.
25. Women and child development.

26. Social welfare.
27. Welfare of weaker section especially scheduled castes and tribes.
28. Public distribution system.
29. Maintenance of community assets.

There are above mentioned powers in the hands of PRI members for the development and progress of the villages.

Finance is a must for execution of all kind of powers. Through this Act local bodies are also made financially free and solvent. In this regard, provision for the establishment of State Finance Commission to allocate adequate resources to the Panchayati Raj Institutions are a welcome step. Amendment provides for the devolution of resources to local bodies and also empowers them to add their own resources according to their need.

The most remarkable and historic feature of the Act is the statutory compulsory reservation of the women and weaker section in the local bodies. The Act deals with the fact regarding these reservations:

(i) According to Article 243(D)—Not less than one-third of the seats will be reserved for women including those for scheduled castes and scheduled tribes. These may be allotted on rotation to different constituencies of a panchayat.

(ii) There would be reservations for women in the seats that have been allotted to scheduled castes and scheduled tribes. Not less than one-third of scheduled caste and schedule tribe seats may be reserved for women.

(iii) Not less than one-third of the total number of seats for the offices of the chairpersons at each level would be reserved for women. This would be rotated among different panchayats at each level.

These features add the process of empowerment of women and disadvantaged classes of the society. It is a historic decision. Because before the enactment of this Act no one was sure about the role of women should play in the reconstruction of village society. Even they had not got their proper share in any political activity. The role played by women is very marginal in politics. Though Mahatma Gandhi had accepted that there will be no development of society without the participation of women in decision making process of the society but it had not attracted women seriously and it is the cause that their participation in decision making bodies, parliament and Vidhan Sabha, is very low.

Women constitute half population of the country. But there is an inequality in all spheres of life. An inequal society cannot nurish its citizens well and perfectly and the vision of Mahatma Gandhi of 'Purna Swaraj' cannot be achieved by neglecting the half population of the society. The Act is based on the philosophy of Mahatma Gandhi.

It can be judged by the result of different Lok Sabha and Rajya Sabha election results. The results show that from the beginning of this globalized era their participation is very low. Women representation in Lok Sabha from 1952 to 2001 has been 8.2 per cent and in Rajya Sabha from 1952 to 2001 it is 10.3 per cent. In Vidhan Sabhas also the situation is the same. Women had got very low representation. Women's political empowerment is so important that there can be no true people's participation in governance, without equal participation of men and women. The goals of development cannot be obtained without women's full and active participation. Credit goes to 73rd and 74th Amendment Acts which have enforced 33 per cent reservation for women in the country and opened a door for their empowerment. In this regard, decision of Bihar government headed by Mr. Nitish Kumar is a landmark in the history of women's development. He had reserved fifty per cent of seats for women in different local body institutions. Bihar is the first state in the country to implement such reservation for women. Around one million women have come forward through this reservation process. Currently almost a million women occupy positions as members and chairpersons in the three tier structure introduced by this Constitutional Amendment Act.

While the constitutional amendment for reservation in the Panchayati Raj Institution gives considerable scope for women to participate in the democratic setup at the grassroots level, in Bihar this little empowerment has not born fruitful. Because election of these institutions are held after a gap of 23 years. In the election of 2001 in Bihar, there were no reservation of the seats of mukhia, sarpanch, pramukh and chairman of the district board. In other states one-third seats in all heads is reserved for women. It is the reason that out of 37 zila parishad seats in 2001 election, only 9 women were elected as the chairpersons in April 2001. But in the election of 2006, 50 per cent reservation had given and single post of mukhia and sarpanch had also come under the limit of reservation, the scenario was totally changed. Out of 381 mukhias in Samastipur district 190 are women and it is same with sarpanch seats also. The chairperson of zila parishad is also a woman, which was not possible before the Act.

According to the 2006 election in Bihar rural women of Bihar have come forward to participate as political representatives of grassroots. It has been observed during study that most of them hail from middle castes or scheduled castes.

Despite the fact that nearly 50 per cent of the electorate are women, and only 7 to 10 per cent of them reach portals of power. They are being used by their male counterparts or family members. So reservation cannot receive the desired result unless giving the real power to women representatives. Although Bihar had many women politicians like Tarkeshwari Sinha, Manorma Devi, Ram Dulari Sinha, Sumitra Devi, Shanti Devi, but they were active in politics not only for their ability but due to their family and wealth status too. These women were either belonged to a political family or were connected with wealth and superior education. The participation of lower income group or downtrodden in society was very low. It is the enhancement of the Amendment Act that these depressed classes of society can make themselves empowered. Now, every class and caste of the society is taking active participation in the political process of the villages through this Act.

Women are the disadvantaged group in rural areas. They are not getting their right in any aspect. It is because the urban middle class are among the planners. These urban middle class women and men cannot understand the problems of rural women. The academics, political parties and different trade unions did not try to rise women's problems. There is a failure of women's movement to attract the problems of all classes of women. There is a need to involve women in playing a significant role in the affairs of the area they inhabited. But it varies from place to place and time to time. Education, family status etc. are not the scale to judge their political participation. For example, the overall literacy rate in Kerala is 90 per cent with 86 per cent women and has a matrilinial tradition yet the representation of women in the state legislative assembly is much lower than Rajasthan, where women live under patriarchal family with a literacy rate of 46.4 per cent. But 73rd Amendment has changed the scenario of the rural environment of the country.

So the political empowerment of women from 73rd Constitutional Amendment has had impact in two ways:— (i) there is a visible improvement in the administration and delivery of services at the Gram Panchayat level and (ii) the amendment has made possible the creation of political space that has enabled women to gain in social stature, confidence and to take revolutionary step against repressive traditions.

It opened a channel for illiterate women members of panchayat who have been afforded opportunities to enter the field of politics through the quota for them in local bodies.

The entry of women in panchayats is yet to be accepted by male members of the society due to reservation. Therefore, they are pressurising their wives and other family members to contest election. After winning the election these women are bound to act as the puppets in the hands of their family members. Because they have no political base.

So it may be concluded that after enactment of the 73rd Amendment Act the chances of the political empowerment of the women in this district had enhanced. Due to *parda* system, maximum numbers of rural women were not confronting the male members. But this barrier is ended. Now both men and women are going equally in the progress of the villages. The Constitutional Amendment for Reservation of Women in the

Panchayati Raj has given considerable scope for women to participate in the democratic set-up at the grassroots level in Bihar. Now women are looking forward to participate in political process. In a large male dominated society, women have still been able to seek a place not behind but beside their male counterparts.

Political awareness of the women has vastly changed during panchayat election 2001. In observation it was found that after assembly election of 2000, women were interviewed about casting of votes and only 31.3 per cent female respondents had cast their vote in the assembly election of 2000. But when the same question was asked after 2001 election of PRIs, the percentage was increased to 74.7 per cent. The following tables show the actual figures.

Table 5.2: Political Awareness of the Respondents in Assembly Election 2000

Sex	No. of Respondens	Number Yes	Percentage	Number No	Percentage
Female	150	47	31.3	103	68.7
Male	50	32	64	18	36
Total	200	79	39.5	121	60.5

Table 5.3: Political Awareness of the Respondents in Panchayati Raj Election 2001

Sex	No. of Respondens	Number Yes	Percentage	Number No	Percentage
Female	150	112	74.7	38	25.3
Male	50	41	82	09	18
Total	200	153	76.5	47	23.5

There is a new political awareness which came after panchayat elections 2001 has not only influenced the upper middle class and caste families but it has also influenced the lower and scheduled caste women. So it may be said that this Act has changed the traditional role of women and took them in the mainstream of the society which was the dream of the Father of the Nation Mahatma Gandhi and his 'Purna Swaraj'.

6

Observations and Findings

From the case studies the following observations can be made.

In terms of secondary data from block offices, we find that villages did not really exhibit any marked difference in figure regarding poverty, literacy, economic conditions under development and so in order to ascertain the degree of political participation of women in Samastipur district, we therefore choose to consider:-

(a) Whether the village was from an open or reserve constituency?
(b) Had any powerful organisation of women in the village?
(c) Whether the family or society interrupts in their political obligation?
(d) What they feel about political empowerment after 73rd Amendment to the Constitution?
(e) The literacy rate of the villages under panchayats.
(f) Is reservation must for women in different political organisations?
(g) Is education necessary for their political empowerment?

In the Kalyanpur block, Kalonzar village and panchayat was visited. 20 representatives from different Panchayati Raj Institution members were interviewed. Smt. Bimla Devi, Tara Devi, Sabu Devi, Kumari Priya were the main respondents. In the village Dighra of same block Smt. Vibha Devi, Malti Devi were interviewed through prescribed questionnaire. In the

Table 6.1: Choice of village/panchayats and their feelings

Block	*Villages*	*Panchayats*	*Women Organisation*	*Role of Family/ Society mixed*	*Feeling about73rd Con.Ame. Act*	*Literacy Rate*	*Importance of Reservation*	*Educational status*	*Economic Conditions*
Samastipur	Chatauna, Samastipur, Jitwarpur, Dudhpura, Musapur, Dariha	Same	2	Society Mixed	Good	42.5	Essential	Good	Mixed
Pusa	Dighra, Kubauli, Pusa-road, Malikaur, Sri Rampur, Birauli	Same	6	Good	Mixed	48.9	Good	Good	Agri-culture good
Kalyanpur	Tira Kalonzar, Ratwara, Birisingpur, Muktapur	Same	5	Satisfactory	Good	37.4	Good	Below	Good
Warisnagar	Dhurlakh, Maniarpur, Rahua, Gohi, Hansa	Same	2	Average	Average	32.5	Not supported	Below	Good
Sarairanjan	ArmauliTiswara, Khalishpur, Kishanpur, Gurma	Same		Good	Good	37.5	Not favoured	Good	Below
Patori	Chaksalem, Chakhaji, Kanasahpur, Undi Jorepur	Same	1	Good	Good	34.7	Good	Below	Below
Dalsingsarai	Ghatho, Kewta, Nagargama, Asinchak, Mathurapur	Same	3	Satisfactory	Good	38.2	Good	Good	Good
Ujiarpur	Satsnpur, Kamla, Karian, Madhopur, Rupauli	Same	2	Average	Good	36.2	Good	Good	Satis-factory
Vidhyapati Nagar	Harpur Boch, Garsisai, Meniarpur, Serpur, Simeri	Same	2	Average	Average	34.2	Average	Below	Satis-factory
Rosra	Rahua, Devdha, Baidhanathpur, Sonupur, Methnnapur	Same	Nil	Average	Mixed	35.3	Average	Below	Good

same way in the Malinagar panchayat of Pusa block, Sulaxna Devi, Roma Kumari, Gaytri Devi all ward members and zila parishad members were interviewed. In all the villages of Kalyanpur except Bashudevpur political awareness in women was found satisfactory after the enactment of the 73rd Amendment Act, 1992.

Likewise villages and panchayats of Pusa block were also visited with the questionnaire Dighra, Patepur, Beroli, Morsand, Harpur, Devpur Mohuadda etc. were visited and found the same result. There most of the seats were reserved for general and scheduled caste women and they were doing their job better in spite of illiteracy and poor political awareness. Though Pusa block is rich in education, but women had not very high literacy rate. It is 48.9 per cent only. During interview one Mosumati Devi had asked many questions regarding women's development. Each at random taken block, was approached with ten to fifteen set of interviews of panchayats and villages with Panchayti Raj Institution members and the general women also. In some villages ex-male representatives were also interviewed for better result. It was discussed on following issues.

Political Awareness

As regard political awareness about Panchayati Raj Institution and 73rd Constitutional Amendment Act, a high level of indifference and unconcern exhibited by women in general and they could not seem to be understood that how political rights and constitutional provisions could make a difference to their overall deprivation. This feeling was found to increase with the geographical isolation of the village, poverty and illiteracy. In the Morsand village of Pusa block, the villagers including the ward members and president who were both women showed very little awareness about the panchayats. The lack of basic idea about the composition, function and other activities of the panchayat were astonishing in this age of information and technology. There is an usual ideology among women that panchayat should be there to solve their problems and provide facilities like electric, water, sources of agriculture, roads, primary education etc. Some of them complained that the president and the ward members were awarding facilities to their relatives and not to those who were needy and helpless. On the other hand in some panchayats president had complained that they had not received power or fund for day-to-day activities or developmental works. So the apathy and indifference to recognise panchayat as a viable mode of political representation was a serious matter of concern. Because without political consciousness and awareness there is no meaning of empowerment. But in Dudhpura panchayat of Samastipur block it showed a strong presence of women activists who are very active and sensitive not only to women's issues but to other socio-political, economic and environmental issues also.

The NGOs and self help groups had created an ambiance of extreme political awareness and financial support to women. Ex-ward member Smt. Anjani Tiwari had accepted that before contesting the election, she was ignorant of the political situation of the panchayat but after being ward member her political awareness and participation had improved. Now she is taking keen interest in the day-to-day working of the panchayat. But in spite of being independent in their views, women basically showed very little interest in political activities, which they either felt is a waste of time and energy. But there are many mukhias and sarpanches who are taking serious actions in different educational plans for children in the panchayat.

In this way it is observed in the field study that political awareness though differs village to village but there is a common issue that proper training and workshops is a must for their political awareness.

Decision Making

In the observation, this aspect is found missing among all spheres of women. Either it is in domestic field, they can make their decision alone. But after the enactment of the 73rd

Amendment Act, many examples of women's own decision were found. Sarita Devi, panch of Nagargama panchayat had proved that once when male members of the panchayat wanted to build a temple in an open field, she had rebelled and forced authorities to build a primary school on it. In another case a road was constructed not to lessen the distance between the village and the highway in Dalsingsarai on the advice of woman member of panchayati raj. Though husbands, father and other family members were considered primary decision makers, but after the Act, this aspect is also changing slowly. Members of self help groups or any NGO like Bina Devi of Armauli village of Sarairanjan block and ex-zila parishad member is very active in politics and she herself took the decision to contest election of Vidhan Sabha. She wants to do something for society, especially for women. She formed many self help groups in the village and made women economically empowered. When she was asked about the problems that she had faced being a woman as zila parishad member, she blamed male dominance in society which makes unable to a woman to hold their own decision. She also complained the non-co-operation of officials to them.

Lady Mukhia of Mahmadpur Koari panchayat of Pusa block Mrs. Amiri Khatoon agreed that she had not much power to take her own decision. The husband performs her duties and his permission was must even to contest the election. In most of the time the women kept away from meeting because either they were not informed or they were busy in their home affairs. Representatives, who won for the second time are able to make their decisions to some extent, but due to constitutional set-up the reservation is made on rotation basis so it is not possible to women to understand the proceedings of panchayat.

Literacy Rate

The literacy rate of female in observation of ten blocks with 50 per cent panchayats and 100 villages, presented the very fading data and it is not up to the mark. It also varies from block to block. In Kalyanpur block panchayats like Jitwaria, Janardhanpur, Barheta, Ratwara, have 46 per cent literacy rate but in Sormar, Srirampur, Bashdevpur, Gopalpur, Jhauri literacy rate is low, i.e. about 36.8 per cent. This is same in Warisnagar, Pusa, and Dalsingsarai, Ujarpur blocks also. There are many factors responsible for low literacy rate among women. This district is a backward district with flood prone areas. Every year flood destroys a vast portion of most of the blocks in the district. Like other districts of north Bihar, this district also depends on agriculture with 92 per cent population. Flood affects agriculture every year, so poverty is a matter of great concern in this district. There are limited number of girls schools in panchayats especially there is hardly a high school in every panchayat and guardians cannot afford to send girls outside the village for many reasons—the sex inequality, *parda* system, dowry system etc. are the main obstacles in the path of their education. Though government has imparted free education but only 14.4 per cent of rural girls visit schools and in high schools dropout rate is much higher. Though incentives, such as free books, cycles, different types of scholarships, uniform, mid-day meal and other facilities are given to them to boost up the participation of girl students in the rural areas and there is improvement also but it is not achieved as was planned. *Parda pratha*, caste system, male dominance in society, problem of law and order etc. are the main reasons for low education rate of girls.

Economic Condition

The development of a society requires full participation by all sections of population and opportunities for full development of the potentialities of women. This is the key note of the U.N. Declaration on the elimination of discrimination against women. But any appraisal of women's economic role has to be separated for specific segments, differentiated by socio-economic and locational characteristics as well as by their capacity to adjustment to the economic process. Samastipur district has agriculture base. Ninety-two per cent population of the district depend upon agriculture. So most of the Panchayati Raj representatives had agricultural background. But it less affects the ideology and principles of the participants. It has generally been found that the success of women candidates depends upon party backing, the campaign strategy adopted and the personality including the family background of candidates. In most of the panchayats, our investigations suggest that experience of social work among women is still considered a qualification for winning election for local bodies. Because the women involved in state politics mostly come from the economic and political elite of states and enter into politics for their supporting backgrounds. Even in the election of mukhia or sarpanch money played vital role in mobilising the people. And there are many complaints found about the use of money, man and muscle power in Panchayati Raj elections also.

Political Empowerment

In the observation it was found that political empowerment of women was very low and slow before enactment of the 73rd Constitutional Amendment Act. Political empowerment is participation in political decision making processes. It can be achieved in three stages—planning, implementation, and delivery. And in all of the stages, we found, it could not be achieved by only physical presence alone. Rather it may be defined by a number of social factors such as illiteracy, unawareness, burden of domestic work, social and family commitments, male centric social values, fear of character assassination etc. It was found that the primary obstacles as delineated by women themselves, which make them weak planners and policy implementers in the local bodies are lack of family and social support, lack of financial support, the cultural barriers male dominated society, lack of education, poverty etc. It was also observed that there was complete ignorance about political rights, constitutional provisions and legal aspects of women empowerment in most of the Panchayati Raj representatives. As far as Panchayati Raj is concerned, the ignorance is very high. Most of the representatives were ignorant about issues like how the funds are being utilised, role of different committees, power and functions of the panchayats. In the same way most of the Panchayati Raj representatives did not have correct information about 73rd Amendment Act. But it is a matter of great happiness that mostly they knew the policy of 50 per cent reservation for women in Panchayati Raj Institutions in Bihar for women. So it was found that most of the elected members had very low level of political awareness and their contribution to developmental activities is almost invisible. The whole developmental works were done by their male partners. Even meetings were also attended by the male members of their family. This is because, being reserved for women seats, they were forced or compelled to contest elections by their family members or husbands. In observation, it was found that after becoming Panchayati Raj Institution's member, some of them had gained political awareness but they could not go free because of family and social interference.

Certain panchayats like Sri Rampur panchayat of Pusa Block or Hansa panchayat of Khanpur block with reserved seats for scheduled caste women showed an impressive full figure. The turnout in last election was more than 68 per cent. But in spite of this, interaction with them proved that as far as sustainability in politics concerned, not single woman had showed interest or capacity in holding political positions. And most of them did not want to contest again. This is because they have come in politics due to family pressure not on their own will.

Aspirations

Elected women in most of the villages are asking for more support by women groups. They demanded more fund and finance to panchayats for developmental works. It is also suggested by the members that the funds should reach them directly. In Rahua panchayat of Warisnagar block, Dhobgama panchayat of Kalyanpur and many others had complained that the officials were not cooperating with them. They demanded more developmental information from the officials.

One thing is very interesting and important that maximum number of women had demanded continuation of reservation for women and advocated for this reservation in Parliament and Vidhan Sabha also. The literate women representatives had also advocated training, workshops, seminars in the local language for information and political orientation, when asked about type of training they were of the view. They advised that it should be based on the fact that how to interact with officials, knowledge of panchayat acts, power of panchayats, rights, duties and powers of the members, working of panchayats, literacy and adult education capacity building, law and regulations regarding women leadership training etc.

In most of the districts of Bihar, women are generally found to be deprived of many social opportunities and infrastructure mainly because of certain entrenched socio-cultural values and also because they have to confine mostly to household activities. Most of the women respondents had indicated that lack of schools, drinking water facility, electric supply, health and sanitation, market, post office, community centres etc. should be major area of concern. Distribution of BPL card is also a controversial issue in villages, women insisted that the deserving people were denied it and beneficiaries are those who are close to mukhia and other officials.

Role of 73rd Amendment in Empowerment of Women

In the whole observation, one thing is common that in all villages and panchayats of the selected blocks women get prestigious status. Though effect of dowry system, cases of atrocities, indifference attitude of society had seen in rural areas but they have autonomy in the domestic affairs. When we explore the political area, the study shows that women are not only hesitant and often discouraged but they also face political indifference along with a lack of proper awareness. It is only in the case of reserved seats that women come forward with the support of their husbands and family members. In all blocks maximum of women spend their time in domestic works, children rearing and other homely affairs. It is their primary duty.

There are traditional customs and institutions, which had never considered it important to make women to participate in community affairs or empower them in economic decision making. In fact socio-cultural impediments push women in the carpet of home and it is common in both classes of women, upper and lower. Level of political awareness of women varies from region to region, class to class and community to community but one thing is also common that all are bound with the culture of their community. We found in our observation that the influence of education and urbanisation are not always uniform. Political awareness of women does not differ significantly between urban and rural areas. In the same way, working women including professionals have greater awareness but this is not always reflected in participation. Nor is there any positive relationship between higher socio-economic status of women and political awareness. The study revealed that political awareness is less among women in the high income groups, who have a negligible interest in politics, though many Panchayati Raj representatives come from a well to do families. Our major observation found one common trend that women were more interested in their general duties than political activities.

Credit goes to 73rd Amendment Act of 1992, which has changed the whole scenario of the political atmosphere of the villages. It has brought bright epoch in the life of deprived eight lakh women, who were brought into the mainsteam of power by reserving 33 per cent seats in Panchayati Raj Institutions for them. The 73rd Amendment Act has made a powerful impact on women by enabling them to enter into the decision making sectors. Out of five lakh villages encompassing more than 600 million people, this amendment has made it possible for 330000 women to enter into politics at the grass-roots level. The percentage of women involved in political activities at the panchayat level by this act is very high. Women candidate have 48.9 per cent population in the country. In Samastipur district it is 46.9 per cent. Before passing the Act no one was sure about the role to be played by the women in the process of development in the society and women themselves. Because the position of women in politics is always marginal not only in Samastipur, Bihar or India but in the whole world. The following table can explain the position clearly.

Table 6.2: Gender Development in Different Countries and India

Country	*HDI*	*Gander Devp.*	*Seats in Parliament*
Canada	1	0.932	22.7
Norway	2	0.932	36.4
USA	3	0.927	12.5
Saint Kits	47	0.792	13.1
Coasta Rica	48	0.789	19.3
Croatia	49	0.790	16.1
Medagaskar	141	0.478	8.0
Nepal	143	0.449	Nil
India	128	0.545	9.00

In the world level, only 10 per cent of the parliamentary position and 6 per cent of the cabinet ministerial posts are occupied by women. Only a few countries like Sweden (40 per cent), Norway (39.4 per cent), Denmark (39.44 per cent) have crossed 30 per cent reservation for women.

Though the Indian Council of Social Science Research has undertaken a major review of the studies conducted in India on different burning issues of politics and society but also was unable to find a chapter on women and their low political participation. Certainly the 73rd and 74th Constitutional Amendment Acts made one to think the role of women in the political processes. The reservation in seats opens the door for women empowerment.

In Bihar local body's election were held in 2000 after a gap of 22 years. There were 116028 seats for Gram Panchayats, 11611 seats for Panchayat Samitis and 1162 seats for Zila Parishads in the election. There are 42934 reserved seats for different Panchayati Raj seats for women, in which Samastipur district has a share of 381 Gram Panchayats and Sarpanches, panchayat samitis, Zila Parishad members. 33 per cent reservation for women in these seats had made a revolutionary change in the political structure of the society. In 2001 election of Panchayati Raj, Mukhia seat was kept out of the purview of reservation, therefore, out of 381 seats only one was won by woman. It was because political and social leadership was a curse to women political elevation. In 2006 election Nitish Kumar government had reserved 50 per cent seats of Panchayati Raj for women and single post of Mukhia and Sarpanches are also reserved. It had changed the political scenario of the district. They are in large number and they have to do a lot of development work.

The situation in different blocks had presented the actual picture in the survey. In Kalyanpur block, there are 4 Zila Parishad seats in which 2 seats are occupied by women. In the same way all the blocks had 50 per cent women members. And after observation, it was found that it had enhanced the political empowerment of the women. But their journey of development is not completed. They have to go ahead. In observation some impediments were also indicated, but they can be managed by proper care. The women representatives of Panchayati Raj have great enthusiasm and vigour, but there is social and political pressure on them which do not give them free hand in discharging their duty honestly and regularly.

It is commonly believed that women's increased presence in local politics will lead to their greater power and influence in policy making. When their participation was observed, it was found that 90.4 per cent of them had contested and won for the first time and when asked about the cause of their entry into politics 56.4 per cent accepted that they were asked to contest by their husbands and family members. A woman panch works in the field, said that her husband forced her to contest and she had not any interest and knowledge of politics. She had not attending the meetings or idea of the functioning of panchayat. So it may be said that reservation which is instrument for empowerment of women can also be used for their exploitation.

In Dalsingsarai and Bibhutipur blocks also panchayat samiti members and lady mukhias had complained that the officials especially BDOs were ignoring the advice of these female members. Punam Devi, mukhia of Birmala Tola panchayat of Ujiarpur had said that she was completely ignored in the panchayat meetings by other male colleagues. In the same way Nilam Devi, deputy mukhia of Chakvaini, Pusa complained us about her demand for women's development was totally refused in meetings. Indu Devi, sarpach of Darsar panchayat, Warisnagar block, Kausalya Devi pramukh of Samastipur, Babita Kiran of Chakvaini panchayat samiti all are of the same view. The situation is worse in that panchayats, where scheduled caste female Panchayati Raj members exist.

So in our observation of different sampling panchayats many findings come up for discussion and proper action. The main findings are:

1. Panchayati Raj Institutions came forward to empower women in the society. It has created a space for women in political participation.
2. It has widened the base of democracy by facilitating the representation of those who are under represented section of the society.
3. It clearly legitimises and asserts the role of women as partners in the public field. This will encourage more women to take up political life as their carrier and shape their priorities accordingly.
4. It has started creating cross hierarchies that have the potential for challenging the hierarchies of patriarchy in the long run.
5. Though women are playing in the hands of their male partners but soon they will be able to assert themselves.
6. Women's entry in politics has brought about qualitative change in her life.
7. It will be able to bring qualitative changes in local politics also. Women can check the increasing corruption in grassroots level.

7

Conclusion

Seeing the participation of women in the institution of democracy is an important feature in global agenda. Because women constitute half of the country's population and are involved in more than half of the economic life of rural India. But their presence in political decision making institutions is very low not in India but in world level also. Only Scandinavian women had 33 per cent share in politics. In world level also women are being neglected in political participation. But the changing political discourse has contributed to the recognition that women must play a greater role in political affairs. Today a strong opinion in world level is building up in favour of increasing women's involvement in the decision making process of the government. Constitutional Amendment Act, 1992 is a bold step in this aspect. Women's empowerment is one of the major objectives of this Act. It provides thirty-three per cent reservation in total number of seats in Panchayati Raj Institutions and chairpersons of all three tiers of Panchayati Raj Institution. Women participation in the Panchayati Raj Institution is essential, not only for ensuring their political participation in the democratic process but also for reaching the developmental goals, for women. Government of India has a major concern for bringing women in the mainstream of development and the year 2001 has been declared as year of women empowerment.

As for women's studies are concerned, the International year for women and the report on status of women in India gave a new turn to the studies of the problems of women and their participation in decision making processes. But in practice it can be possible only through Constitutional Amendment Act, 1992, which had not only given power of decision making to the women but also gave recognition to them. The present study is an attempt to find out the real participation of rural women, especially in Samastipur district and trace out the problems and hurdles in their path.

Many works had been done on women's participation in political process, but there is a lack of original work based on data and empirical study. Most of these works are based on the role of women in the freedom movement, different studies on women in the electoral process. In my opinion, the present study will be a practical study based on original data of different at random selected panchayats in the Samastipur district, which can focus the various aspects of women and Panchayati Raj System in Samastipur district.

There are seven chapters in this research project. The first chapter introduces the problem, need, methodology field observation of the subject. There is a detail description of the facts regarding women empowerment through Panchayati Raj Institution. It is explained in detail that how and why, women's participation in the political process of a country is the need of the hour. It is a serious problem that how women can properly participate in the political process of a country? Because different data from different Lok Sabha and State Assemblies elections show their low participation, below ten per cent. But Constitutional Amendment Act, 1992 had made an easy way for women by reserving 33 per cent seats for them in decision making processes.

Many studies had done on women's participation but not a block and panchayat level study in totally rural environment was done on micro level. Therefore, a micro study of at random selected panchayats was done to examine the actual political participation of rural women in the political process.

For the study of the 'Emerging Political Role of Women Through PRIs in Samastipur District', two simple methods were chosen—questionnaire method and interview and observation method. Data was collected from two sources—primary sources and secondary sources. For primary sources, interviews of the selected panchayat members and other people were conducted and secondary sources were collected from books and journals from different libraries, newspapers, magazines etc. through these processes, it was observed that this Act had changed the political scenario of the panchayats with 33 per cent reservation for women. It had made them strong in political decision making, who are very enthusiastic and full of vigour. They are not only taking part in decision making processes but also in the development and progress of their panchayats also. So the objective of the Panchayati Raj Act to emerge the political role of women had achieved to a large extent.

The second chapter deals with Importance and Utility of Local Self Government in general and PRIs in particular in democratic set-up of a country. Mahatma Gandhi had said that 'the greater the power of the panchayats, the better for the people'. Jawaharlal Nehru also accepted that 'the progress of our country is bound to go up with the progress of our villages. If our villages make progress, India will become a strong nation and nobody will be able to stop its onward march. So India's Independence must begin at the bottom.' There are some areas of development which are strictly local in character and which requires local knowledge, local initiative and local action. Therefore, participation of local people in these institutions are a must for development. Local government strengthens the foundation of democracy and consolidation of democracy by forging the much desired linkage between people at grassroots and the national elites at central or state level. The basic idea behind local government is to involve people in their own development and to train local leadership to assume higher responsibilities and serve people with efficiency. So it is also studied in this research project.

Then in the third chapter of the research study, two sub-tittles are discussed:

(a) Bihar: Political Atmosphere and Women.
(b) The Land of Mithila: Physical Structure, Political Atmosphere and Women.

Different data show that the situation in Bihar was not in favour for women's political participation before 73rd Amendment Act. Criminalisation of politics and Politicalisation of criminals are one of the serious factors, responsible for low political participation of women in politics in Bihar. Besides, male dominance in society, women's inferior status, illiteracy among women, lack of self-confidence, lack of decision making capacities, *Parda Pratha,* customs and traditions are responsible for lower participation of women in Bihar in general and region of Mithila in particular.

In the second part of the chapter historical, geographical and political aspects of Mithila have been discussed. Because Samastipur falls in this region and without the knowledge of its demographic features no research can be made perfectly. Though, Mithila has a glorious historical aspect of women's empowerment. Bharti the wife of famous scholar Mandan Mishra, who had defeated Shankracharya in religious discourse, but after independence due to geographical and traditional reasons women participation became very low in social and political activities. This is the reason that in Samastipur district, out of 10 Legislative Assembly Seats only one is occupied by women. There was no lady M.P. in the district since independence. In Lok Sabha a woman M.P. had won from Ujiarpur seat in Samastipur district. In the field of education this district is below the literacy rate of nation. Due to social and cultural rituals—*parda* system, dowry system, child marriage, polygamy, male dominance in society, women's position is not governable in the society. It is discussed in the chapter through different data collected in sampling villages.

The fourth chapter deals with the political participation of women in Samastipur district. Samastipur district is a combination of Mithila and Tirhut culture. Areas of Pusa, Tajpur are guided by Muzafferpur culture while Kalyanpur, Khanpur, Warisnagar, Rosra, Shivajee Nagar from Darbhanga Culture. In the same way Bibhutipur, Dalsingsarai, Ujiarpur, Sarairanjan etc. are guided by the culture of Begusarai. So the situation varies from panchayat to panchayat, but one thing is clear that women are treated as second class citizen in whole of the district. Before the enactment of 73rd Act women's position was not satisfactory in politics, after this Act, election was held in 2001 and 2006. In 2006 election the present government had reserved 50 per cent seats for women. Now out of 381 mukhias and sarpanches 50 per cent are women and out of 51 zila parishad members 25 are women in the district. The chairman and vice chairman of zila parishad are also women. But due to unavoidable reasons, they are not enjoying their political right independently. There are 42 per cent literacy rate in women in this district. Due to illiteracy, officials are not cooperating them. They are also unable to understand the technical aspects of administration. Male dominance in society compels them to follow the decision of their family members regarding meetings and developmental work. They cannot take their own decision.

The 73rd Amendment Act had changed the scenario on the whole. The fifth chapter of this research project deals with this fact. It may be said that this Act is a milestone in the way of women's assuming leadership and decision making positions. Through this Act women's entry in village political system would ensure change in the political system of the village, the familial and social perceptions of the role of women and development of grassroots leadership in women. At the Gram Sabha and panchayat level a new leadership would emerge which is expected to administer better administration and would provide constructive thinking in village development and progress. Prior to 73rd Amendment women occupied negligible percentage in Panchayati Raj system. Now with this constitutional provision, there are eight lakh women, who have been elected to different posts from the chairpersons of Zila Parishads to Gram Panchayat members and they are performing their duties carefully and honestly. There are 29 important subjects, and most of them are related to the problems and welfare of children and women. Women are participating in the developmental role of panchayats including the preparation of plans of economic development, and social justice at the village and intermediate levels and district level. A study of ten blocks of Samastipur district revealed that reservation of seats for women in Panchayati Raj bodies has provided an opportunity for their formal involvement in the development and political process at the grassroots level and enabled them to influence the decision making process in the local government. They got the power to express their opinion or grievances on socio-economic problems of the society. It certainly makes them enable to emerge as effective leaders for social change among rural women.

In the sixth chapter observations and findings are explained. Through the implementation of 73rd Amendment Act, political awareness had increased in rural surroundings. When asked about their political participation 80 per cent women accepted that before the enactment of the Act they were unknown to the political process of the local politics, but after reservation through the Act, they were taking keen interest in their political participation. When asked that did they want to be elected again, 84.6 per cent replies were in affirmative, 42.8 per cent had accepted that they want to contest M.L.A. and M.P. election on reserved seats. They were seen happy with their post because they were getting respect both at home and society. But the quality of decision making is found missing in all the women members except very few. Though 73rd Amendment Act had given the power of decision making to them but examples shown in the observation that they are still dependent on their male members for decision making process. Out of fifty respondents from various panchayats only 11 were taking their own decision occasionally, rest depend upon their family members. 64.2 per cent of them accepted that they could not understand the matters of politics, 30.4 per cent could understand but due to the pressure of family and husband did not make their own decisions, only 9.2 per cent were of the opinion that they could really understand the matters.

In the matter of policy making and leadership experiences, 90.9 per cent of them had contested and won for the first time. So they were less aware of local politics. The sarpanch and mukhia of Rahua panchayat of Warisnagar block, both are women and both had committed that they were not familiar with local atmosphere.

Elected women in most of the villages are now asking for more support from women's organisations. Their political empowerment can be imagined from the figure that 91.3 per cent of them demanded more fund and financial support to panchayats for development works. It was also advised that these funds should reach directly. In chapter seventh, the findings and observation are mentioned, which are based on data from primary sources, through fieldwork. Though secondary sources have also been explored. In the observation and findings it was stated that there was a large demand of such reservation at parliamentary and assembly level also. The respondents were asked whether there should be reservation in parliament and assemblies, 89.5 per cent were in favour of the reservation.

So the main objective of this project was to find out the level of political awareness, through 73rd Amendment Act, 1992 in Samastipur district of Bihar. It was found in the observation that before the enactment of the Panchayati Raj Act, 1992, the level of political awareness and participation was very low in this district. But after enactment of the law and fifty per cent reservation for women through this Act, had enhanced the political awareness of women. So it may be concluded that fifty per cent reservation in Panchayati Raj Institutions had changed the political role of women in rural environment, so it should be extended in Lok Sabha and Legislative Assemblies also, so that the political empowerment of women can be achieved to large extent.

APPENDIX-I

प्रश्नावली

(Questionnaires)

निर्देश

नीचे कुछ प्रश्न दिये गये हैं जिसका उत्तर आपको 'हाँ' या 'नहीं' में देना है। कोई भी प्रश्न सही या गलत नहीं है। आपके जो उत्तर होंगे वही सही माने जायेंगे। आपके उत्तर को गोपनीय रखा जायेगा। जिस प्रश्न से आप सहमति प्रकट करते हैं उसमें हाँ को टिक (√) कर दें तथा जिस प्रश्न से आप असहमति प्रकट करते हैं उसमें ना (×) कर दें।

परिचयात्मक विवरणी

(क) नाम   लिंग   उम्र

(ख) पिता/अभिभावक का नाम

(ग) शैक्षणिक योग्यता - शिक्षित / अशिक्षित

(घ) निवास- (क) ग्राम   पंचायत

(ख) नगर   वार्ड

(ङ) पेशा- (i) नौकरी

(ii) व्यवसाय

(iii) कृषि

(iv) अन्य

(च) परिवार में सदस्यों की संख्या

(छ) मासिक आय

(ज) जाति-(उच्च जाति/पिछड़ी/अति पिछड़ी/हरिजन)

(झ) आर्थिक स्तर-(उच्च वर्ग/मध्यम वर्ग/निम्न वर्ग)

(झ) धर्म-(हिन्दू/मुस्लिम/सिख/अन्य)

प्रश्न

1. क्या आप सोचते है कि महिलाओं को शिक्षित होना चाहिए? हाँ/नहीं
2. क्या आप सोचते हैं कि शिक्षा से जागरूकता घटी है? हाँ/नहीं
3. क्या आप सोचते हैं कि राजनीतिक जागरूकता महिलाओं के लिए आवश्यक है? हाँ/नहीं
4. क्या आप सोचते हैं कि राजनीतिक जागरूकता से सामाजिक जागरूकता हो सकती है? हाँ/नहीं
5. क्या आप सोचते हैं कि राजनीतिक जागरूकता से आर्थिक निर्भरता घटेगी? हाँ/नहीं
6. क्या आप सोचते हैं कि राजनीतिक जागरूकता से महिलाओं का सबलीकरण बढ़ा है? हाँ/नहीं
7. क्या आप सोचते हैं कि राजनीतिक जागरूकता से आर्थिक निर्भरता बढ़ेगी? हाँ/नहीं
8. क्या आप सोचते हैं कि आरक्षण से महिलाओं की राजनीतिक भागीदारी बढ़ी है? हाँ/नहीं
9. क्या आप सोचते हैं कि राजनीति में महिलाओं की भागीदारी संतोषजनक नहीं है? हाँ/नहीं
10. क्या आप सोचते हैं कि महिलाओं को परिवार में ही रहना चाहिए? हाँ/नहीं
11. क्या आप सोचते हैं कि राजनीति में आरक्षण से महिलाओं का राजनीतिक सबलीकरण हुआ है? हाँ/नहीं
12. क्या आप सोचते हैं कि राजनीतिक भागीदारी से महिलाएँ अपने हित पर सोचेगी? हाँ/नहीं
13. क्या आप सोचते हैं कि महिला के सुरक्षा के लिए कानूनों को प्रभावी बनाने का प्रयास होगा? हाँ/नहीं
14. क्या आप सोचते हैं कि राजनीतिक भागीदारी में महिलायें परिवार के लिए भी सोचेंगी? हाँ/नहीं

15. क्या आप सोचते हैं कि कानून बनाने मात्र से ही महिला मजबूत नहीं हो जायेगी? हाँ/नहीं
16. क्या आप सोचते हैं कि कानून के निर्माण में समस्त समाज की सहायता मिलनी चाहिए? हाँ/नहीं
17. क्या आप सोचते हैं कि महिला हित पर समाज को गंभीरता से सोचना चाहिए? हाँ/नहीं
18. क्या आप सोचते हैं कि आधी आबादी की उपेक्षा समाज के लिए कलंक है? हाँ/नहीं
19. क्या आप सोचते हैं कि समाज की सोच बदलने में महिला की भूमिका महत्वपूर्ण है? हाँ/नहीं
20. क्या आप सोचते हैं कि महिला में आत्म सोच की प्रवृत्ति को बढ़ावा देना चाहिए? हाँ/नहीं
21. क्या आप सोचते हैं कि महिलाओं को अपने स्वास्थ्य के प्रति जागरूक/सतर्क होना चाहिए? हाँ/नहीं
22. क्या आप सोचते हैं कि महिलाओं को अपने व्यक्तित्व के विकास के प्रति सजग होना चाहिए? हाँ/नहीं
23. क्या आप सोचते हैं कि महिलाओं की पुरुषों पर निर्भरता कम होनी चाहिए? हाँ/नहीं
24. क्या आप सोचते हैं कि महिलाओं को स्वयं निर्णय लेने की क्षमता को विकसित करना चाहिए? हाँ/नहीं
25. क्या आप सोचते हैं कि परिवार के सदस्यों को महिलाओं के शैक्षणिक क्षमता के विकास में सहयोग करना चाहिए? हाँ/नहीं
26. क्या आप सोचते हैं कि महिलाओं को भोग की वस्तु समझने की परम्परा को बदलना चाहिए? हाँ/नहीं
27. क्या आप सोचते हैं कि महिलाओं को पुरुषों के समान सुविधा मिलनी चाहिए? हाँ/नहीं
28. क्या आप सोचते हैं कि महिलाओं को पुरुषों के समान वेतन नहीं मिलना चाहिए? हाँ/नहीं
29. क्या आप सोचते हैं कि महिलाओं को पारिवारिक निर्णय में भागीदार बनाना चाहिए? हाँ/नहीं

30. क्या आप सोचते हैं कि महिलाओं को घर से बाहर जाकर खरीदारी करनी चाहिए? हाँ/नहीं
31. क्या आप सोचते हैं कि परिवार के पुरुष सदस्यों के द्वारा महिलाओं को अनावश्यक दबाव दिया जाता है? हाँ/नहीं
32. क्या आप सोचते हैं कि पंचायती राज संस्थाओं में भागीदारी से महिलाओं में जागरूकता बढ़ी है? हाँ/नहीं
33. क्या आप सोचते है कि आरक्षण द्वारा ही महिला सबलीकरण संभव है? हाँ/नहीं
34. क्या आप सोचते है कि महिलाओं के लिए 33% आरक्षण उचित नहीं है? हाँ/नहीं
35. क्या आप सोचते हैं कि बिहार में 50% आरक्षण महिला सबलीकरण के लिए एक महत्वपूर्ण कदम है? हाँ/नहीं
36. क्या आप सोचते हैं कि महिलाओं के लिए सीटों का आरक्षण विधान सभा में भी होना चाहिए? हाँ/नहीं
37. क्या आप सोचते हैं कि महिलाओं के लिए आरक्षण संसद में भी होना चाहिए? हाँ/नहीं
38. क्या आप सोचते हैं कि सिर्फ आरक्षण से महिलाओं का सबलीकरण नहीं होगा? हाँ/नहीं
39. क्या आप सोचते हैं कि आरक्षण द्वारा महिलाओं का आर्थिक उत्थान हुआ है? हाँ/नहीं
40. क्या आप सोचते हैं कि आरक्षण की प्रथा समाप्त होनी चाहिए? हाँ/नहीं
41. क्या आप सोचते हैं कि आरक्षण का आधार आर्थिक होना चाहिए? हाँ/नहीं
42. क्या आप सोचते हैं कि सिर्फ आरक्षण से महिलाओं की स्थिति सम्मानजनक नहीं हो सकती है? हाँ/नहीं
43. क्या आप संविधान के 73वें संवैधानिक संशोधन विधेयक के अंतर्गत महिला से संबंधित तथ्यों से अवगत हैं? हाँ/नहीं
44. क्या आप संविधान के 73वें संशोधन विधेयक द्वारा महिला एवं दलित आरक्षण को उचित मानते हैं? हाँ/नहीं

45. क्या आप सोचते हैं कि संविधान के नये संशोधन द्वारा 33% आरक्षण को 50% करना चाहिए? हाँ/नहीं
46. क्या आप सोचते हैं कि रीति-रिवाज एवं परंपरायें महिला सबलीकरण में बाधक हैं? हाँ/नहीं
47. क्या आप सोचते हैं कि समाज के परंपरागत रीतिरिवाज में परिवर्तन नहीं होनी चाहिए? हाँ/नहीं
48. क्या आप सोचते हैं कि महिलाओं को भी विकास का समान अवसर मिलना चाहिए? हाँ/नहीं
49. क्या आप सोचते हैं कि भ्रूण हत्या पर कानून के अतिरिक्त सामाजिक दृष्टिकोण भी बदलना चाहिए? हाँ/नहीं
50. क्या आप सोचते हैं कि राष्ट्र के विकास के लिए महिला सबलीकरण आवश्यक नहीं है? हाँ/नहीं
51. क्या आप सोचते हैं कि स्थानीय स्वशासन में भाग लेकर महिलायें सबल महसूस कर रही हैं?

APPENDIX-II

साक्षात्कार
(Interview)

निर्देश

नीचे कुछ प्रश्न दिये गये हैं जिसका उत्तर आपको 'हाँ' या 'नहीं' में देना है। कोई भी प्रश्न सही या गलत नहीं है। आपके जो उत्तर होंगे वही सही माने जायेंगे। आपके उत्तर को गोपनीय रखा जायेगा। जिस प्रश्न से आप सहमति प्रकट करते है उसमें हाँ को टिक (√) कर दें तथा जिस प्रश्न से आप असहमति प्रकट करते है उसमें ना (×) कर दें।

परिचयात्मक विवरणी

(क) नाम लिंग उम्र

(ख) पिता/अभिभावक का नाम

(ग) शैक्षणिक योग्यता - शिक्षित / अशिक्षित

(घ) निवास- (क) ग्राम पंचायत

(ख) नगर वार्ड

(ङ) पेशा- (i) नौकरी

(ii) व्यवसाय

(iii) कृषि

(iv) अन्य

(च) परिवार में सदस्यों की संख्या

(छ) मासिक आय

(ज) जाति-(उच्च जाति/पिछड़ी/अति पिछड़ी/हरिजन)

(झ) आर्थिक स्तर-(उच्च वर्ग/मध्यम वर्ग/निम्न वर्ग)

(झ) धर्म-(हिन्दू/मुस्लिम/सिख/अन्य)

प्रश्न

1. क्या आपके विचार में पंचायत के सुचारू ढंग से कार्य करने से जनतंत्र सुदृढ़ होगा? हाँ/नहीं
2. पंचायत के सही ढंग से कार्य करने के लिए जो कानून बने हैं उसकी जानकारी आपको है? हाँ/नहीं
3. क्या आपके विचार में पंचायत के कार्यकरण के लिए बने कानून पर्याप्त हैं? हाँ/नहीं
4. क्या आपके विचार में तिहत्तरवें संवैधानिक विधेयक द्वारा 33% महिला आरक्षण सबलीकरण की दिशा में सही प्रयास है? हाँ/नहीं
5. क्या बिहार की तरह अन्य प्रदेशों में भी महिलाओं को 50% आरक्षण देना चाहिए? हाँ/नहीं
6. क्या 33% महिला आरक्षण से महिला सबलीकरण हुआ है? हाँ/नहीं
7. क्या आपके विचार में महिला सबलीकरण के लिए बने कानून पर्याप्त नहीं है? हाँ/नहीं
8. क्या आपके विचार में समाज के सोच में परिवर्तन आवश्यक है? हाँ/नहीं
9. क्या आपके विचार में महिलाओं को द्वितीय वर्ग का नागरिक समझना उचित है? हाँ/नहीं
10. क्या आपके विचार में महिलाओं की शिक्षा व्यवस्था प्राथमिक स्तर पर नहीं होनी चाहिए? हाँ/नहीं
11. क्या आपके विचार में महिलाओं एवं पुरुषों को एक समान देखना चाहिए? हाँ/नहीं
12. क्या आपके विचार में महिला को समाज के मुख्य धारा से जोड़ना चाहिए? हाँ/नहीं
13. क्या आपके विचार में महिला के बाहर निकलने से परिवार प्रभावित नहीं हुआ है? हाँ/नहीं
14. क्या आपके विचार में महिला के बाहर निकलने से पारिवारिक टकराहट नहीं बढ़ी है? हाँ/नहीं
15. क्या आपके विचार में राजनीति अधिकारों से महिला उद्दंड होंगी? हाँ/नहीं
16. क्या आपके विचार से स्थानीय स्वशासन में भाग लेकर महिला सबल हुई हैं? हाँ/नहीं

Bibliography

Books

Adamson, N., Briskin, L., *Feminist Organizing for Change*, Oxford, Oxford Univeristy Press, 1988.

Agnew, U., *Elite women in Indian Politics*, Bombay, Delhi, Calcutta, Bangalore, Vikas, 1979.

Agnimitra, N., Women in Panchayats Empowerment or Illusion, 1996, *Gandhi Marg* (Jan.-March) Vol. 17, No. 4, pp. 442-44.

Agrwal, R.C., *Constitutional Development and National Movement of India*, S. Chand, 2007.

Ajay Kuar, K. Kumari, *Rural Women in Bihar*, Janak Pub., Patna, 2005.

Alva Margaret, Whither Indian women, seminar spet. , No. 457, pp. 33-41, 997.

Arun Rashmi, Role of women in Panchayati Raj—The Administrator, *CAP*. June Vol. X 21 pp. 115-116.

Athreya Ub, *Women's Participation in Panchayati Raj*, 1998.

Bashan, A. L., *Wonder that was India*, 2007.

Besai, N. and Patel, V., *Indian women change and challanges in the international decade*, 1975, Popular, Bombay.

Bharadwaj, R.K., *Urban Development in India*, 2005.

Bhatnager, R., Violence against women's, *The Times of India*, 4th Aug., 1998.

Boserup, Ester, *Women's Role in Economic Development*, New York, St. Mertin Press, 1970.

Brown, H., *Women Organisation*, London, 1992, Routledge.

Bulback, C., *One World Women's Movement*, Delhi, Ajanta Pub., 1988.

Chamber, R., *Rural Development: Principles, Policies and Management*, Sage Pub., 1986, New Delhi, pp. 18-19.

Chatterjee B., *Women and Politics in India,* 2004.

Cottrell J., Women Humen Rights and Enviorment, *The Administrator Cap.,* June Vol. XXXIX p. 89.

Dhar, A.R., Women's Participation in Politics, *The I.J.P. Adm.* Jan-Mar. 2001, p. 2531.

Friedle, E., *Women and men, An Anthropological View,* Holt, Rinehart and Winston, 1975, New York.

Gounder, A.M., *Investment in Women's Education,* 2003.

Government of India, *Economic Survey 2000-01.*

Government of India, *Ninty Five Years Plan 1997-2002,* Vol. 2.

Government of India, *Report on the Committee of Panchayati Raj Institutions,* New Delhi, Ministry of Agriculture, 1978, pp. 8-9.

Gowda, S. Govinda, *Women in Panchayati Raj Institution, A Case Study in Karnataka.*

Gandhi, M.K., *Women Ist Education,* Navajivan Publication, Ahmedabad, 1958.

Gandhi, M.K., *Women and Social Injustice,* Navjivan Publication House, Ahmedabad, 1958.

Hire Meathu. Women in Grassroot, *Politics Social Welfare,* May, Vol. 44, No. 2, pp. 7-14, 1997.

Jain, P. and Mahan, R., *Women Images,* Jaipur, 1996.

Jhamtani, Amita, Rural Women: The Powerless Partners in Development, *Kurukshetra,* Aug., Vol. XLIII, No 11, pp. 19-21.

Joshi, R.P., *Panchayati Raj in India: Emerging Trends Across the States,* Jaipur, Rawat 2002, pp. 161-64.

Kalba, C., *Women and Development* (Vol. I-VII), New Delhi, 1991, Discovery.

Kumari, U.I., Empowerment of Women and Rural Development, Serial Pub., New Delhi, 2005.

Khan, M.A., *Status of Rural Women in India,* Uppal Pub. House, New Delhi, 1982.

Kumari, K., *Problem of Rural Women: A case study of Mithilanchal Region,* 2002.

Lama, H.D., *Women in Local Government, A study of Maharashtra,* New Delhi, Concept, 1983.

Mathew, G., *Panchayati Raj : From Legislation to Movement,* New Delhi, p. 130.

Moti Pal, Women in Panchayats, *Economic and Political Weekly,* Jan., p. 150, 1998.

Mani, Kaya P., *Women in Panchayati Raj Structure,* New Delhi, Gian Pub., 1989.

Mathew, D., *Good Governance: Initiatives in India,* Prentice Hall of India, New Delhi, 2003.

Mathew, G., Women and Panchayati Raj with Reservation Insured Participation, *S. Welfare,* Vol. 42 No. 56, pp. 32-34, 1995.

Menon, L., *Women Empowerment and Challanges of Change,* New Delhi, Kanisk Pub., 1998.

Mishra, S., Women and 73rd Constitutional Amendment Act, *A Critical Appraisal of Social Action* (Jan.-March) Vol. 47, pp. 16-29.

Mohanthi, B., Panchayati Raj, 73rd Constitutional Amendment and Women, *Eco. and Pol. Weekly,* 30 Dec., p. 3346, 1995.

Mukhopadhyay, M., *Education in India: Dynamics and Development.* Shipra Pub., 2007.

Narayan, U., Women in Panchayats : The Partli Ahead, *Mainstream,* Vol. XXXIV, No. 50, pp. 11-12, 1996.

Nanivedekar Medha, Reservation for women, *Eco. and Pol.* Weekly, Jul. Vol XXXIII, No. 28, pp. 1815-16.

Narain, G.R., National Conference on Panchayati Raj and Women, *Social Welfare,* Vol. XXXVI, No. 3, pp. 4-7, 1989.

Nehru, J., *Discovery of India.*

Palanithurai, G., Report of Empowerment of Panchayati Raj Institution, 1998.

Parda, S., Women in Rural Local Government, *Kurukshetra,* April, Vol. XLIII, No. 7, pp. 103-105.

Patow, S., *Women Political Elite: Search for Identify,* Jaipur, Printwell, 1994.

Paylee, M.V., *Constitutional Government in India,* S. Chand, New Delhi, 2005.

Paylee, M.V., *India's Constitution,* S. Chand, 2006.

Pillai, J.K., *Women and Empowerment,* 1995.

Pramanik, R.M., *Gender Inequality and Women Empowerment*, Abhijeet Pub., New Delhi, 2006.

Rukmani, K., Women's studies in India, *W. News*, ALU. Vol. 38.

Rao, M.K., Empowerment of women in India, Serials Pub., New Delhi, 2005.

Reddy, R.R., *Empowerment of Women and Ecological Development*, Serials Pub., New Delhi, 2002.

Ray, B., *Globalisation and Women in India : A Women's Studies Perspective.*

Reddy, K.S., *Inequality Problem in Men and Women*, Praja Shakti Book House, 1997.

Shukla, D.K., Panchayati Raj and Emerging Women Leadership, *Social Welfare*, Jan.-Mar., Vol. 46, pp. 77-91.

Subramanyam, K., *Women and Law*, Asish Law House, Hydrabad, 1991.

Sharma, Kumud, Gender Environment and Structure Adjustment, *EPW*, 1994.

Status of Women in India: A Synopsis of the Report of N.C.

Sharma, K., Women's Political Power 1994 and The State, 2006.

Salgaonkar, S.P., Women's Political Power and The State, 2006.

Singh, Kartar, *Rural Development: Principles, Policies and Management*, Sage Pub., 1986.

Uma, R., Women and Development: *The Indian Journal of Labour Economics*, Vol. 34, No. 4, pp. 18-20, 1991.

UNESCO, *Women and Development*, Paris, 1959.

UNESCO, *Educational Planning and Human Resource Development*, Paris, 1967.

Verma, U.P., *Modern Indian Political Thought*, Laxmi Narain Pub., Agra, 1959.

Vidya, K.C., Political Empowerment of Women Act: The Grassroots, New Delhi, Kankhan Pub., 1997.

Yasoda, S., *Women Employment in India*, Allied Pub., Chennai, 1993.

Yadav, R.S., *Adult Education : Conception Theory and Practice*, Asia Pub., Ambala, 2002.

Journals and Magazines

Bandyopadhyaya, B., Gender and Governance in *Indian Eco. and Pol. Weekly*, July 29, 2000.

Golcla, S., *Report of the Committee on the Status of Women in India*, Dept. of Social Welfare, New Delhi.

Gandem, N. S., Development of women and children in Rural Areas : An Apprasail, *Kurukshetra*, pp. 45-47, 1999.

Government of India, *Economic Survey 2000-2001.*

Human Devp. Report (1995), New York, Oxford University Press.

Padmanabhan, B. S., Women Empowermnet in Farm Sector, *Yojana*, Jan., 2001, Vol. 45, No. 1, D. 47.

Ramaswamy, U., Women and Development, *The Indian Journal of Labour Eco.*, Vol. 34, No. 4, 1991.

Sujata, D. H., Poltical Participation of Women and the Dilectics of 73rd Amendment, *I.J.P.S.* Vol LXVII, 2 April-June, 2006.

Taneja, A., Gandhi, Women and the National Government 1920-27. *The Indian Journal of Pub. Admn.* Vol. 21, No. Jan.-Mar. 2005.

The Hindu, Environmental Survey 2002.

Kurukshetra, Regular.

Yojana, Regular.

Grih Sobha, Regular.

Femina, Regular.

Garg, S., State Panchayati Raj Institutions: Financial Relations, *Administrative Change*, Vol. XXV, No. 1, Jul.-Dec. 1997.

Journal of Rural Development, Vol. 16, No. 4, Oct.-Dec. 1997.

Omvedt, Gail, Women and Rural Revolt in India, *Journal of Peasant Studies*, Vol. 5, 1997.

Riberio, Circumventing the Axis, *The Teligraph*, New Delhi, 12 May, 1995.

Ojha, M., Women and Crime, *Times of India*, Patna Ed. 14 Oct. 2005.

Pandey S., Political Empowerment of Women: A Case Study, Orissa, *Journal of Rural Devp.*, Vol. 1156, No. 4 Oct.-Dec. 1997.

Index